Applied Virtualization Technology

Usage Models for IT Professionals and Software Developers

Sean Campbell
Michael Jeronimo

PRESS

ISBN 0-9764832-3-8

Publisher: Richard Bowles
Editor: David J. Clark
Content Architect: Stuart Goldstein
Text Design & Composition: Horizon Interactive
Graphic Art: Kirsten Foote (illustrations), Ron Bohart (cover)

Library of Congress Cataloging in Publication Data:

Printed in the United States of America

10 9 8 7 6 5 4 3 2 1

First printing, May 2006

To Kim, Ryan, and Josh for the time that they put aside in order to allow me to write this book. Through this book and the others I have authored they have been a strong source of support and affirmation and for that I am very grateful.

—Sean

To Frank DeRemer. Thanks for taking a chance years ago on a kid right out of college and getting my career started on the right track. Your generosity and integrity have been an inspiration to me.

—Michael

Contents

Chapter 3   **Impact of Virtualization   67**

Chapter 4   **Software Development: Developers   81**

Chapter 5   Software Development: Testing   103

Chapter 6   **Software Development: Marketing, Educating, and Selling   127**

Preface

Virtualization technology can impact an organization at many different levels. It can provide benefits in day-to-day tasks as well as cost savings and increased productivity that can be seen at more strategic levels. One of the things that has been lacking, however, in the discussion about virtualization is a book that illustrates where virtualization can be applied to software development organizations and IT organizations without limiting the discussion to one particular vendor's toolset.

Before deciding to implement a paradigm-shifting technology like virtualization and making the commitment to incorporate it into your software development efforts and/or IT structure, it is important to understand the variety of effects virtualization technology can have on your organization.

This book provides a solid and thorough treatment of the various use cases in which virtualization can be applied within an organization and literally provides over 70 such use cases spread across software development and IT scenarios.

This book also provides some context early on of how Intel® Virtualization Technology is a significant component of virtualization efforts for Intel and others moving forward.

We both hope that, upon finishing this book, you will be able to confidently chart a path for making good use of virtualization technologies to the benefit of your organization.

Intended Audience

Perhaps you are new to virtualization and are wondering what all of the fuss is about. This book will help you to understand why virtualization technology is so significant and why we are so excited about its possibilities. Or, you may already be using virtualization, perhaps by consolidating multiple virtual servers onto a single hardware platform, but are wondering about other ways virtualization can save you time and money. In either case, we hope that this book sparks your imagination by providing new ways to use virtualization that you hadn't considered before. We also hope that you can realize some of these usage models in your work environment and that they provide you with significant benefit.

Acknowledgements

A book is always a labor of love for which the reward extends out over a period of time. But during the development of the book there are many that helped in the creative process, with editing, and with support and affirmation. We would like to thank the good folks at Intel Press who have been very gracious in their help and support during the development effort. This includes but is not limited to Stuart Goldstein, David Clark, Richard Bowles, and others that are part of the process of getting this book to market but we were not fortunate enough to meet.

We would also like to thank those at Intel who reviewed the manuscript and provided us with important feedback and suggestions: Paul Barr, Steve Bennett, Clyde Hedrick, Arun Krishnaswamy, Felix Leung, Ed Lisle, Fernando Martins, Sunil Saxena, Chad Taggard, Glenn Quiro, and Richard Uhlig. In addition, Michael Pretz of Daimler Chrysler and Joel Wycoff of Wypro helped us with review and validation of the book.

Comments and Questions

We hope that we have produced a book that you find useful. Please let us know how we can improve it in future editions and printings. You can reach us by sending an e-mail to Intel Press at intelpress intel.com. For more information about the book and Intel Press, please visit the Intel Press Web site at http://www.intel.com/intelpress/.

Chapter 1

Introduction to Virtualization

*You cannot step twice into the same river, for other waters are
continually flowing in.*
—Heraclitus

Virtualization is one of the more significant technologies to impact computing in the last few years. With roots extending back several decades, today its resurgence in popularity has many industry analysts predicting that its use will grow expansively in companies over the next several years. Promising benefits such as consolidation of infrastructure, lower costs, greater security, ease of management, better employee productivity, and more, it's easy to see why virtualization is poised to change the landscape of computing.

If you're getting ready to move into the virtualization environment or just thinking about it, this book will help you sort through the software solutions that exist today and help you gain an understanding of how to put virtualization technology to use. A variety of use case scenarios for IT and software development offer you a detailed look at how virtualization technologies can reap benefits in the workplace. Later chapters discuss the limitations of virtualization today in regards to IT and software development scenarios. The book concludes with a look into the possible future of virtualization.

But what exactly is virtualization? The term is used abundantly, and often confusingly, throughout the computing industry. You'll quickly discover after sifting through the literature that virtualization can take on different shades of meaning depending on the type of solution or strategy

1

being discussed and whether the reference applies to memory, hardware, storage, operating systems, or the like. It is perhaps best to first aim for a general definition of the term itself and to explain how the term will be used within the scope of this book.

So to open this chapter, a definition of virtualization is in order.

Virtualization Defined

Virtualization refers in this book to the process of decoupling the hardware from the operating system on a physical machine. It turns what used to be considered purely hardware into software. Put simply, you can think of virtualization as essentially a computer within a computer, implemented in software. This is true all the way down to the emulation of certain types of devices, such as sound cards, CPUs, memory, and physical storage. An instance of an operating system running in a virtualized environment is known as a virtual machine. Virtualization technologies allow multiple virtual machines, with heterogeneous operating systems to run side by side and in isolation on the same physical machine. By emulating a complete hardware system, from processor to network card, each virtual machine can share a common set of hardware unaware that this hardware may also be being used by another virtual machine at the same time. The operating system running in the virtual machine sees a consistent, normalized set of hardware regardless of the actual physical hardware components. Technologies such as Intel® Virtualization Technology (Intel® VT), which will be reviewed later in this chapter, significantly improves and enhances virtualization from the perspective of the vendors that produce these solutions.

With a working definition of virtualization on the table, here's a quick mention of some of the other types of virtualization technology available today. For example, computer memory virtualization is software that allows a program to address a much larger amount of memory than is actually available. To accomplish this, you would generally swap units of address space back and forth as needed between a storage device and virtual memory. In computer storage management, virtualization is the pooling of physical storage from multiple network storage devices into what appears to be a single storage device that is managed from a central console. In an environment using network virtualization, the virtual machine implements virtual network adapters on a system with a host network adapter. But again in the context of this book virtualization refers to the process of utilizing virtual machines.

Terminology

Individual vendors often choose terminology that suits their marketing needs to describe their products. Like the nuances of the virtualization technologies, it's easy to get confused over the different terms used to describe features or components. Hopefully as virtualization technology continues to evolve and as more players enter the marketplace, a common set of terminology will emerge. But for now, here is a list of terms and corresponding definitions that this book uses.

Host Machine

A host machine is the physical machine running the virtualization software. It contains the physical resources, such as memory, hard disk space, and CPU, and other resources, such as network access, that the virtual machines utilize.

Virtual Machine

The virtual machine is the virtualized representation of a physical machine that is run and maintained by the virtualization software. Each virtual machine, implemented as a single file or a small collection of files in a single folder on the host system, behaves as if it is running on an individual, physical, non-virtualized PC.

Virtualization Software

Virtualization software is a generic term denoting software from vendors such as VMware and Microsoft that allows a user to run virtual machines on a host machine.

Virtual Disk

The term refers to the virtual machine's physical representation on the disk of the host machine. A virtual disk comprises either a single file, as is the case with Microsoft† Virtual PC† and Virtual Server†, or a collection of related files, as is the case with VMware† Workstation†, ESX Server†, and GSX Server†. It appears to the virtual machine as a physical hard disk.

One of the benefits of using virtual machine architecture is its portability whereby you can move virtual disk files from one physical machine to another with limited impact on the files. Subsequent chapters illustrate various ways in which this can be a significant benefit across a wide variety of areas.

Virtual Machine Additions

Virtual machine additions increase the performance of the guest operating system when compared to running without the additions, provide access to USB devices and other specialized devices, and, in some cases, to higher video resolutions than without the additions, thus offering an improved user interface experience within a virtual machine. The additions also allow the use of customizations such as shared folders, drag-and-drop copy and paste between the host and virtual machines and between virtual machines, and other enhancements.

One particularly useful enhancement is the ability of the mouse pointer's focus to naturally move from the virtual machine window to the host machine's active application windows without having to physically adjust it each time the window changes. This allows you to interact with the virtualized operating system as if it were nothing more than another application window, such as a word processing program running on the host machine.

Typically virtual machine additions are installed immediately after installing the virtual machine's operating system using the user interface that the virtualization software vendor provides for launching virtual machines. The installation process is short for virtual machine additions, generally lasting only a few minutes, and requires a reboot of the virtual machine.

Shared Folders

Most virtual machine implementations support the use of shared folders. After the installation of virtual machine additions, shared folders enables the virtual machine to access data on the host. Through a series of under-the-cover drive mappings the virtual machine can open up files and folders on the physical host machine. You then can transfer these files from the physical machine to a virtual machine using a standard mechanism such as a mapped drive.

Shared folders can access installation files for programs, data files, or other files that you need to copy and load into the virtual machine. With shared folders you don't have to copy data files into each virtual machine. Instead, all of your virtual machines access the same files through a shared folder that targets a single endpoint on the physical host machine.

Some virtual machine vendors also support a solution where you can copy and paste small numbers of files and/or folders from one machine to another using the drag-and-drop operation to place them on the open window for the virtual machine.

Virtual Machine Monitor

A virtual machine monitor is the software solution that implements virtualization to run in conjunction with the host operating system. The virtual machine monitor virtualizes certain hardware resources, such as the CPU, memory, and physical disk, and creates emulated devices for virtual machines running on the host machine. An overview of emulated devices is presented later in this chapter. For now, it is important to understand that the virtual machine monitor determines how resources should be allocated, virtualized, and presented to the virtual machines running on the host computer. Many software solutions that exist today utilize this method of virtualization. Figure 1.1 illustrates the concept of the virtual machine monitor.

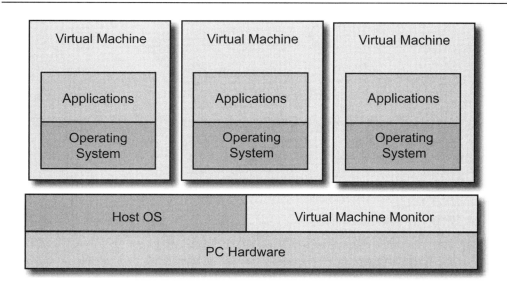

Figure 1.1   Virtual Machine Monitor Architecture

Hypervisor

In contrast to the virtual machine monitor, a hypervisor runs directly on the physical hardware. Vendors that use the hypervisor solution include VMware (in their ESX Server product) and XenSource. Microsoft also has stated that it plans to implement a hypervisor solution.

The hypervisor runs directly on the hardware without any intervening help from the host operating system to provide access to hardware resources. The hypervisor is directly responsible for hosting and managing virtual machines running on the host machine. However, the implementation of the hypervisor and its overall benefits vary widely across vendors.

Figure 1.2 illustrates the concept of a hypervisor.

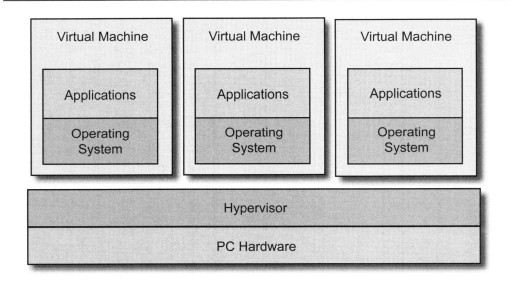

Figure 1.2   Hypervisor Architecture Overview

Paravirtualization

Paravirtualization, currently used by the Xen[†] product, involves modifying the operating system before it can be allowed to run in the virtualized environment as a virtual machine. Thus its use requires an open source operating system whose source is publicly available.

Virtual Machine Isolation

While not strictly a technical term, the concept of virtual machine isolation is important to understand in order to grasp portions of the discussion that follows throughout the rest of this book. Virtual machines are essentially isolated from one another in the same way that two physical machines would be on the same network. A virtual machine's running operating system has no knowledge of other virtual machines running on the same machine. In some cases, the operating system itself has no way of knowing that it is running in a virtualized environment either. This isolation and separation has important benefits that forthcoming chapters will review in detail.

History of Virtualization

Before we place a foot firmly into the realm of virtualization technologies that exist today, it's worthwhile to take a step back into history to explore the origin of virtualization within the mainframe environment. This is important because virtualization in its current incarnation is not a completely new technology and has roots in some past efforts.

From the 1950s to the 1990s

The concept of virtual memory dates to the late 1950s when a group at the University of Manchester introduced automatic page replacement in the Atlas system, a transistorized mainframe computer. The principle of paging as a method to store and transmit data up and down the memory hierarchy already existed but the Atlas was the first to automate the process, thereby providing the first working prototype of virtual memory.

The term virtual machine dates to the 1960s. One of the earliest virtual machine systems comes from IBM. Around 1967, IBM introduced the System/360 model 67, its first major system with virtual memory. Integral to the model 67 was the concept of a self-virtualizing processor instruction set, perfected in later models. The model 67 used a very early operating system called CP-67, which evolved into the virtual machine (VM) operating systems. VM allowed users to run several operating systems on a single processor machine. Essentially VM and the mainframe hardware cooperated so that multiple instances of any operating system, each with protected access to the full instruction set, could concurrently coexist.

In the mid 1960s IBM also pioneered the M44/44X project, exploring the emerging concept of time sharing. At the core of the system architecture was a set of virtual machines, one for each user. The main machine was an IBM 7044 (M44 for short) and each virtual machine was an experimental image of the 7044 (44X for short). This work eventually led to the widely-used VM/timesharing systems, including IBM's well-known VM/370.

The concept of hardware virtualization also emerged during this time, allowing the virtual machine monitor to run virtual machines in an isolated and protected environment. Because the virtual machine monitor is transparent to the software running in the virtual machine, the software thinks that it has exclusive control of the hardware. The concept was perfected over time so that eventually virtual machine monitors could function with only small performance and resource overhead.

By the mid 1970s, virtualization was well accepted by users of various operating systems. The use of virtualization during these decades solved important problems. For example, the emergence of virtual storage in large-scale operating systems gave programs the illusion that they could address far more main storage (memory) than the machine actually contained. Virtual storage expanded system capacity and made programming less complex and much more productive.

Also, unlike virtual resources, real system resources were extremely expensive. Virtual machines presented an efficient way to gain the maximum benefit from what was then a sizable investment in a company's data center.

Although hardware-level virtual machines were popular in both the research and commercial marketplace during the 1960s and 1970s, they essentially disappeared during the 1980s and 1990s. The need for virtualization, in general, declined when low-cost minicomputers and personal computers came on the market.

Although not the focus of this book, another type of virtual machine, Sun Microsystems' Java Virtual Machine (JVM) and Microsoft's Common Language Runtime (CLR), deserve a place on the historical timeline and are worth mentioning here. The key thing to understand though is that these machines do not present a virtual hardware platform. But due to the potential confusion between this type of virtual machine and the virtual machines covered in this book a brief overview is in order to clear up these differences. These virtual machines emerged during the 1990s and extended the use of virtual machines into other areas, such as software development. Referred to as simulated or abstracted machines, they are implemented in software on top of a real hardware platform and operating system. Their beauty lies in their portability. In the case of JVM, compiled Java programs can run on compatible Java virtual machines regardless of the type of machine underneath the implementation.

Figure 1.3 outlines the relationship between a JVM or the CLR and the host operating system.

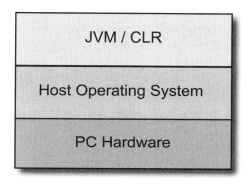

Figure 1.3   Runtime Virtual Machines

The Reemergence of Virtualization

The 1990s saw an explosion in the number of servers used throughout the enterprise. However, while their numbers continued to grow many were underutilized in the workplace. Placing more than one application on a single server often was not a viable option even though that one application might use only a fraction of the server's available resources. Server proliferation presented deployment, update, and support challenges as well as issues with security and disaster recovery. Organizations soon realized that while waste and costs were escalating, productivity and efficiency were plummeting. The question became, "how do we consolidate our servers?" The answer was to use virtualization technology.

While the past several years have seen the re-emergence of virtualization, vendors have faced significant complications in developing the software to allow others to virtualize operating systems and applications. The advent of Intel VT has removed or significantly reduced some of these complications. Intel recognized the re-emergence of virtualization and began working with VMM developers, implementing hardware assists in Intel processors and chipsets, and driving specifications to improve virtualization in the future.

Challenges with the IA-32 Architecture and Software-Only Virtualization Solutions

So far the landscape of virtualization seems to be trouble free. But there is a crucial problem and that concerns the original IA-32 architecture. It wasn't designed for virtualization. Intel processors were designed primarily to run a single instance of the operating system. So on systems that use Intel architecture, virtualization is presently a software-only solution. Here is a look at the problem and the various approaches used to solve the problem before the benefit of using Intel VT became available.

IA-32 Architecture and Privilege Levels

Intel processors provide protection based on various rings or privilege levels, numbered 0, 1, 2, and 3. The privilege level, 0 being the highest, determines what actions a specific process can perform. For example, memory mapping can be executed only in privilege level 0. In contrast, end-user applications run in privilege level 3. Software running in a lower-numbered privilege level can exercise control over software running at a higher-numbered privilege level. Most IA-32 software uses only privilege levels 0 and 3.

Some of an operating system's components must run at privilege level 0 in order to have unlimited access to the underlying CPU. Similarly, in a virtualized system the virtual machine monitor (VMM) must ring in privilege level 0. The VMM must also create the illusion to the guest operating system that it, too, is running in ring 0. But the VMM cannot allow a guest operating system such control because doing so might modify the VMM's code and data or give the guest operating system access to privileged instructions.

Before the availability of virtualization software, privilege levels would have been of little concern. To get around the conflict with privilege levels, the virtualization software relocates the guest operating system to another ring—a technique known as *ring deprivileging*. Deprivileging is accomplished using one of two models. If the system uses the ring 0/1/3 model, the virtualization software deprivileges the guest operating system to privilege level 1. This allows the guest operating system to properly control its applications by locating them in privilege level 3. In the 0/3/3 model the guest operating system is moved to privilege level 3 where it runs at the same privilege level as its applications. With either model, the VMM has privilege level 0 all to itself.

Unfortunately, deprivileging creates a new set of virtualization challenges. The VMM must constantly monitor the activities of the guest operating systems to trap attempts to access the hardware and certain system calls. It must execute these calls itself and emulate the results. For example, when software runs at a privilege level other than the one for which it was written, as in the case with the guest operating system, a problem referred to as *ring aliasing* can arise. Certain instruction calls authorized for use outside privilege level 0 can return a value that contains the current privilege level. The guest operating system is able to read the return value and determine that it is not running at privilege level 0. A conflict within the guest operating system could develop. However, since the call is a valid operation for an application running at privilege levels greater than 0, the VMM is unable to detect and provide the proper fix for this operation.

Another problem arises when the guest operating system, thinking it has control of the state of the CPU, makes a valid request for the state of the CPU. The CPU state returned is the true state of the CPU controlled by the VMM, not the simulated CPU state of the guest operating system. These values are in conflict and could cause execution failure.

The VMM that is in charge of the CPU must switch the context of the guest operating system process. A guest operating system is not generally written to support context switching and may store important data in hidden locations. When the VMM attempts to save the context, this information can be lost. Restoring the complete context of the guest operating system would not be possible and the guest operating system would produce an execution failure. There are numerous other scenarios with adverse impacts.

Addressing the Virtualization Challenges

To address the virtualization challenges, designers of virtual machine monitors have developed two approaches: Paravirtualization and binary translation.

Paravirtualization

Briefly discussed earlier this solution requires changes to the source code of the guest operating system, especially the kernel, so that it can be run on the specific VMM. Paravirtualization can be used only with operating systems that can be modified, such as Linux. Xen uses this method in part to support its virtualization scenarios.

Binary Translation (or Patching)

With this approach the VMM makes changes to the binaries of the guest operating system as it is loaded into the virtual machine. This on-the-fly solution extends the range of operating systems that can be supported as the operating system does not need to be modified to support this approach but comes with higher performance overhead than VMMs that use paravirtualization. This approach also requires a greater effort in some ways on the part of the designer of the VMM. Microsoft and VMware use this method to support their virtualization scenarios.

Intel® Virtualization Technology (Intel® VT)—Solving the Privilege Problem

Intel Virtualization Technology, a series of hardware-based processor and chipset innovations, delivers support to address some of the problems with software-only solutions. It enables VMMs to run off-the-shelf operating systems and applications and allows guest software to run at its intended privilege level, thereby eliminating the need for paravirtualization and binary translation. Intel VT includes VT-x support for IA-32 processor virtualization and VT-i support for the Itanium® architecture. Here is a high-level look at the extensions to the IA-32 architecture.

Virtual Machine Extensions (VMX) Operations

VT-x augments the current IA-32 architecture with a new mode of CPU operation: VMX, which stands for virtual machine extensions. The VMM runs in VMX root operating level, which is fully privileged. Guest operating systems run in VMX non-root operating level. The key point is that both forms of operation support all four ring levels. The guest operating systems run within their expected ring levels and each thinks it controls the CPU; that is, the entire machine. The guest operating system in constrained, however, not by privilege level, but because it runs in VMX non-root operating level.

Two transitions are associated with VMX. These commands associated with these transitions pass control back and forth between the VMM and the guest operation systems:

- ■ VM entry—VMM- to-guest transition, which enters VMX non-root operations

- ■ VM exit—guest-to-VMM transition, which enters VMX root operations.

With the VM entry command, the guest operating system can execute VMX non-root operations. When the guest operating system passes control back to the VMM with the VM exit command, the VMM returns executing its privileged VMX root operations again. The virtual machine control structure is a new data structure that manages VM entries and VM exits.

The VT-x technology, initially code-named Vanderpool, is currently shipping in some Intel Pentium® and Intel Xeon® processors. At the time of this publication, VT-x is expected to be supported broadly in both platforms, as well as in mobile processors, in mid 2006.

Virtual Machine Benefits

Reducing hardware and software needs, improving performance and scalability, and reducing downtime are key factors in managing costs in today's companies. Virtual machines provide the means for companies to achieve these goals. Here is a brief overview of the benefits you can expect to gain using virtual machines. These benefits will be covered in depth later in this book in richer scenarios as well as in the context of other scenarios.

- ■ Virtual machines allow more efficient use of resources by consolidating multiple operating environments on underutilized servers onto a smaller number of virtualized servers.

- ■ Virtual machines make the manageability of systems easier. For example, you do not need to shut down servers to add more memory or upgrade a CPU.

- ■ The complexity of overall administration is reduced because each virtual machine's software environment is independent from the underlying physical server environment.

- ■ The environment of a virtual machine is completely isolated from the host machine and the environments of other virtual machines so you can build out highly-secure environments that are tailored to your specifications. For example, you can configure a different security setting for each virtual machine. Also, any attempt by a user to interfere with the system would be foiled because one virtual environment cannot access another unless the virtualization stack allows this. Otherwise, it restricts access entirely.

■ You can migrate old operating systems for which it is difficult to obtain appropriate underlying hardware for a physical machine. Along these same lines, you can run old software that has not been, or cannot be, ported to newer platforms.

■ You can run multiple, different operating systems from different vendors simultaneously on a single piece of hardware.

■ Because virtual machines are encapsulated into files you can easily save and copy a virtual machine. You can quickly move fully configured systems from one physical server to another.

■ Virtualization allows you to deliver a pre-configured environment for internal or external deployment scenarios.

■ Virtual machines allow for powerful debugging and performance monitoring. Operating systems can be debugged without losing productivity and without having to set up a more complicated debugging environment.

■ The virtual machine provides a compatible abstraction so that all software written for it will run on it. For example, a hardware-level virtual machine will run all the software, operating systems, and applications written for the hardware. Similarly, an operating system–level virtual machine will run applications for that particular operating system, and a high-level virtual machine will run programs written in the high-level language.

■ Because virtual machines can isolate what they run, they can provide fault and error containment. You can insert faults proactively into software to study its subsequent behavior. You can save the state, examine it, modify it, reload it, and so on. In addition to this type of isolation, the virtualization layer can execute performance isolation so that resources consumed by one virtual machine do not necessarily affect the performance of other virtual machines.

Forthcoming chapters explore these benefits within the context of scenarios that use virtualization for software development and IT.

Multi-Core Technologies and Virtualization Technologies

One of the primary applications of virtualization technology involves running more than one operating system at the same time on one physical machine. Multiple operating systems are, in particular, necessary in development and testing situations where engineers must develop software simultaneously on different operating systems. They are also very common in IT scenarios where legacy operating systems need to run side by side with more modern systems. However with virtualization technology, an installed operating system such as Microsoft[†] Windows[†] is not designed to share hardware resources, such as processor, memory, disk space, network, and video, with other operating systems running at the same time on the same physical machine. To sidestep this constraint, the user had to, prior to the advent of virtualization, dual-boot (or tri-boot, and so on) the machine between the different operating systems such as Windows XP and Linux[†].

Dual booting gives the user the flexibility of using multiple operating systems but at the significant disadvantage of having to shut down one operating system completely before using another. In order to share core data files and documents, the user must store them in a location available to each operating system regardless of which one is currently booted and in active use, which further reduces productivity and increases complexity. While this is viable in some contexts it slows down the process of interacting with the host machine and in some contexts is simply not a viable solution as will be outlined in later chapters. In addition processing power must be wholly applied to the execution of one operating system or other and cannot be easily split across all the operating systems you might want to run concurrently on the same machine. Virtualization makes it possible to remove all of these limitations.

By contrast, each virtualized operating system takes a portion of available resources such as CPU, memory, and physical disk and uses them for its own user-specified tasks. However, sharing the same physical resources that previously would have been dedicated to one physical machine comes at a cost. The host machine that is running these virtualized operating systems must have more resources than were previously allocated to a single machine.

A possible solution to this dilemma may lie in the emergence of increased processing power. With today's emphasis on multiple core architecture and Hyper-Threading Technology, these processors can be best utilized when placed in an environment where virtualization is in heavy use. The additional core(s) these processors provide can be dedicated to individual virtualized operating systems to allow the optimum scale out of resources. Additional benefits such as separating defined user tasks into given virtualized operating systems can allow for more secure or hardened dedicated virtualized operating systems all operating on the same piece of physical hardware. The use of virtualization makes it possible to take full advantage of new processor architectures and processors that go from dual-core to quad-core, eight-core, and beyond.

Hardware Utilization—Possible Performance Impacts

Virtualizing your infrastructure or even a small number of machines can have enormous benefits, but it can also affect the performance of your server, workstation, or mobile machine hardware even with advances such as multi-core processors. It is important to understand some of the tradeoffs that occur at the hardware level with virtualization. This section outlines them on a component-by-component basis. More specific use cases are covered in later chapters.

Physical RAM, CPU, hard disk space, and networking all play a role is determining whether a host machine is prepared to run a virtual machine-based application. Properly preparing your host machines prior to running virtual machines on them will help you achieve better stability, scalability and long-term performance for your virtual machines. When selecting a host, you'll need to ensure that it meets the virtual machine application's minimum hardware requirements and further that enough resources, particularly memory, are available for the number of virtual machines you want to run simultaneously on the host.

Here is a breakdown of the various hardware components that are the usual bottlenecks and what can be done to prevent them.

CPU

The CPU is one of the more significant bottlenecks in the system when running multiple virtual machines. All of the operating systems that are running on the host in a virtual machine are competing for access to the

CPU. An effective solution to this problem is to use a multi-processor or, better, a multi-core machine where you can dedicate a core or more to a virtual machine. The technology to assign a given core to a virtual machine image is not yet fully provided by current virtualization vendors but is expected to be available in the near future. In the absence of a multi-core processor, the next best step is to find the fastest processor available to meet your needs.

Memory

Memory also can be a significant bottleneck but its effect can be mitigated, in part, by selecting the best vendor for your virtualization solution because various vendors handle memory utilization differently. For example, Microsoft Virtual PC allocates all memory at the moment the virtual machine launches whereas VMware's Workstation product swaps and allocates memory amongst machines if the memory is currently not in use.

Regardless of the vendor you chose, you must have a significant amount of memory—one that is roughly equivalent to the amount you would have assigned to each machine if they were to run as a physical machine. For example, to run Windows XP Professional on a virtual machine, you might allocate 256 megabytes (MB) of memory. This is on top of the 256 MB recommended for the host computer, assuming Windows XP is the host.

This can mean in many cases that a base machine configuration comes out to approximately 1–2 gigabytes (GB) of memory or perhaps many more gigabytes for a server-based virtualization solution.

You can easily change memory configuration for a guest operating system that is virtualized. Typically this change is done from within the virtualization software itself and requires only a shutdown and restart cycle of the virtual machine to take effect. Contrast this process with the requirement to manually install memory on each physical machine and you can see one of the benefits of virtualization technology.

Physical Disk

With 250-GB drives and up on desktops and 100-GB drives on laptops becoming the norm at the time of this printing, when it comes to virtualization, overall disk space utilization for each virtual machine isn't as great a concern as is the intelligent utilization of each physical drive. An additional important point to consider is the rotational speed of the drive in use. Because you may utilize multiple virtual machines on a single drive the rotational speed of the drive can have a dramatic affect on performance with greater drive speeds. For the best performance across most of the virtualization products today, consider implementing multiple disk drives and using the fastest drive possible, in terms of its rotation speed, for each drive.

One way to boost performance of a virtualized solution beyond just having a faster drive is to ensure that the host machine and its associated operating system have a dedicated physical hard drive, and that all virtual machines or potentially each virtual machine has a separate physical hard disk allocated to it.

Network

Network utilization can also present bottleneck issues, similar to those with memory. Even though the virtual machine doesn't add any significant amount of network latency into the equation, the host machine must have the capacity to service the network needs of all of the running virtual machines on the host machine. However as with memory you still need to apply the appropriate amount of network bandwidth and network resources that you would have if the machines were running on separate physical hardware.

You might need to upgrade your network card if you are running multiple virtual machines in an IT environment and all machines are experiencing heavy concurrent network traffic. But in most desktop virtualization scenarios you will find that the network is not the problem. Most likely the culprit is the CPU, disk, or memory.

Device Emulation

An important point to consider when running in a virtualized environment is that the devices from the host are virtualized, not 1-to-1 mappings of the underlying host machine's hardware. The cost to virtualize a host's 256-MB video card with a dedicated graphics processor and a number of other potential peripherals would be too expensive to support in terms of host machine CPU utilization on today's hardware. Thus, the different virtualization software vendors have created a set of base hardware that is virtualized and it is this hardware that the operating system running in a virtualized environment detects and runs on.

Table 1.1 lays out some of the distinctions between the Microsoft and VMware products in particular.

Table 1.1   Device Emulation for Microsoft Virtual PC and VMware Products

Feature	Microsoft Virtual PC[†]	VMware Workstation, GSX[†] and ESX[†] Server
BIOS	American Megatrends	Phoenix
CD-ROM	Readable	Re-writeable
DVD-ROM	Readable	Re-writeable
Maximum Memory	4GB (64 GB Virtual Server)	4GB (64 GB ESX and GSX)
Chipset	Intel 440BX	Intel 440BX
Parallel Port	LPT1	LPT1 and 2
Serial Port	COM 1 and 2	COM 1,2,3,4
Sound	SoundBlaster[†] (none on Virtual Server)	SoundBlaster
Video	8MB S3 Trio (4 MB on Virtual Server)	SVGA
IDE Devices	4 (none on Virtual Server)	4
SCSI	No (Adaptec 7870 on Virtual Server)	LSI 53c1030 and BusLogic BT-358
NIC	Intel 21141 Multiport 10/100	AMD PCnet-PCI[†] II 10/100 (1000 as well on ESX/GSX)
PCI Slots	5	6

Development and IT scenarios are likely to experience the limitations imposed by device emulation. Chapter 7 explores this important issue in more depth.

Vendor Solutions and Intel VT

Vendors' plans to build solutions based on Intel VT have not been widely made available. But some information has been publicly disclosed to date and this section summarizes these disclosures.

Microsoft's Solutions Supporting Intel VT

Microsoft's plans at the present time are hard to discern in full. On the client side, Microsoft has not publicly indicated that they have plans to support virtualization in the Windows Vista release timeframe. However a host of changes that support Intel VT are planned for the Virtual Server product.

Microsoft's future plans, as they have been publicly discussed to date in various presentations and papers, focus on the development of a hypervisor-based solution that integrates with a small parent partition running Windows. This solution is expected to approximately coincide with the release of Longhorn Server.

Microsoft's hypervisor-based solution also differs in one key respect from other Hypervisor implementations at least as they exist today. Drivers are not integrated into the hypervisor portion of the virtualization stack but reside in the operating systems that are running in the virtualized environment. This approach provides more flexibility in terms of compatibility with existing drivers and future drivers, but at the cost of requiring increased integration between the hypervisor and the running virtual machines and their associated operating systems.

The release of a server-based virtualization product as described above will also support Intel VT, although the specifics are not available at this time.

Microsoft also plans to add what they are currently calling "Windows Enlightenments" that allows Windows to be aware that it is running as a guest operating system. This will consist of a series of API calls that allow a developer to determine whether a given application is running on top of an operating system that is currently virtualized and running as a guest operating system.

VMware Solutions with Intel VT Integration

At this time VMware has not announced their future plans for supporting Intel VT beyond their recent support for it in their Workstation 5.5 release, as well as their recent announcement to support it in their ESX Server product sometime in the 2006 to 2007 timeframe.

Open Source Xen Solutions with Intel VT Integration

Several companies, including XenSource, Red Hat, Novell, and Virtual Iron, have announced plans for products based on Xen. XenSource has also been working to develop solutions supporting Intel VT. While the exact roadmap for these solutions remains unclear, XenSource has been active in demonstrating builds of Xen that make use of platforms with Intel VT.

Conclusion

Virtualization technology while not new is growing at a significant rate in its use on servers and desktop machines and has long ago lost its connection to mainframe systems alone. While challenges do exist, such as the unification of terminology, the development of even more robust software solutions, and the implementation of greater device virtualization support, virtualization is still poised to make a significant impact on the landscape of computing over the next few years.

Virtualization in the form of hardware virtualization, which is the focus of this book, provides a host of benefits to the company or individual who wishes to take advantage of it. Subsequent chapters will spend significant time laying out these benefits as a series of use cases.

The next chapter takes a closer look at what VMware, Microsoft, and XenSource bring to the table in terms of feature sets and implementation details. Providing information on these current software capabilities will help set the stage for the deeper discussions of use cases for virtualization that follow in later chapters.

Chapter 2

Virtualization Products

Any sufficiently advanced technology is indistinguishable from magic.
—Arthur C. Clarke

The three major sources for virtualization technology featured in this book, VMware, Microsoft, and Xen, offer established virtualization products that share common features. These features include the use of virtual hardware and support for running multiple guest operating systems on a single host machine. Each technology approaches the challenges of virtualization with different tools and configuration options.

This chapter surveys these vendor solutions, highlighting both their similarities and their differences to help provide a framework for understanding some of the larger vendors in the virtualization arena. This base context can then form the basis for understanding some of the use cases discussed in later chapters.

Creating a Virtual Machine

One of the unique aspects of creating a virtual machine is how easy it is from an end-user perspective of the software compared to creating a physical machine. In order to showcase some of the steps, this section illustrates that process with one particular vendor. Other vendors follow similar steps and have similar if not identical options in their products.

The overriding goal here is not to provide an exhaustive discussion of the options available or a how to but to give you a glimpse at the process of creating a virtual machine if you have not gone through the process before with a given vendor's toolset.

Each virtualization product provides its own mechanism for creating a virtual machine. The virtual machine creation options in each will be similar to the options offered by the VMware New Virtual Machine Wizard, discussed below. The VMware New Virtual Machine Wizard walks you through the following configuration decisions:

- Virtual machine format
- Guest operating system
- Virtual machine name
- Number of processors
- Amount of RAM allocated to the virtual machine
- Type of network connection
- Type of I/O adapter
- Disk type, disk capacity, and virtual disk file name (if using a virtual disk)

Virtual Machine Format

As each virtualization product matures, new features sometimes require changes to the format of the virtual machine's configuration files and virtual disk files. With the release of version 5 of VMware Workstation and VMware Server, for example, VMware introduced a new format. Current versions of VMware can run virtual machines using the format from prior versions of VMware, but these legacy virtual machines cannot take advantage of the full features of version 5.0 and higher of VMware Workstation and VMware Server, including important features such as snapshots and cloning.

Guest Operating System

Because of differences in the ways that various guest operating systems access hardware, the virtualization product must either make allowances for these differences or modify the guest operating system itself. In the VMware example, VMware runs unmodified operating systems and must know what guest operating system you intend to run in your virtual machine. In this way, VMware can account for differences in the ways that each guest operating system accesses hardware and other resources on the host system. While VMware and Microsoft Virtual PC require no modification to the guest operating system, other virtualization products that use paravirtualization, such as Xen, require modifications to the guest operating system.

Note

> While VMware and Microsoft Virtual PC do not require changes to the guest operating system, both provide special drivers and tools to improve performance and user interface integration between the guest and host operating systems. See the discussion of VMware Tools and Microsoft's Virtual Machine Additions later in this chapter.

Virtual Machine Name

The control application on the host machine must have a mechanism for identifying each virtual machine. The VMware console uses the virtual machine name you specify when you create the virtual machine. This name is not necessarily the same one as the file name of the virtual disk file or the machine name that the guest operating system uses.

Number of Processors

You can configure the virtual machine with multiple processors, regardless of the number of processors in the physical host machine. In the VMware example, this feature helps a developer using VMware Workstation to test multiprocessor-enabled applications on host machines with a single processor.

Random Access Memory (RAM)

Virtual machines must be configured with a specific amount of memory. Figure 2.1 shows the VMware Memory dialog box, which provides suggestions for minimum, recommended, and maximum amounts of RAM for each supported guest operating system. Base your decision on how much RAM to assign to the virtual machine on the amount of physical memory installed on the host machine and the memory needs of the applications and services to be installed on the virtual machine.

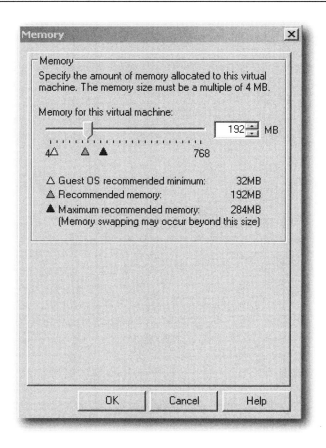

Figure 2.1   Configuring Virtual Machine Memory

Network Connection Type

Each virtualization product offers a variety of options for how to treat the virtual network interfaces. In VMware, you can configure each virtual machine with one or more network interfaces. Figure 2.2 shows the Network adapter dialog box, which offers four types of virtual network connections.

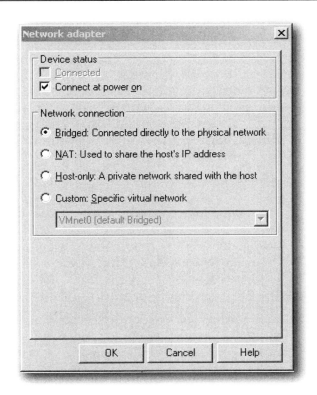

Figure 2.2   Types of Network Connections

■ *Bridged.* A bridged network connection maps the virtual machine directly to a physical network adapter. The virtual machine appears to other network devices as if the virtual operating system is running on a physical machine. If the guest operating system, for example, uses DHCP to obtain an IP address, the DHCP server on the physical network sees the virtual machine as just another DHCP client. Other machines on the network can connect to the virtual machine just as though the virtual machine is a physical machine attached to the network.

■ *NAT.* A Network Address Translation (NAT) connection provides access to the physical network, allowing multiple virtual machines to use a single physical adapter and IP address. With NAT, other physical machines on the network do not have direct access to the virtual machine, but the virtual machine can connect to most network resources. For example, virtual machines running Windows 2000 or XP can use the Windows Update feature to download updates as long as the host machine has a working Internet connection. In a development environment with limited valid IP addresses, NAT provides a way to connect virtual machines to the network without wasting valuable IP addresses, and can provide some security benefits by restricting external network devices from initiating connections to the virtual machine.

■ *Host-only.* A host-only connection allows communication between both the virtual machine and the host machine and between multiple virtual machines running on the same host. Host-only networking isolates the virtual machine from the physical network. Driver updates must be downloaded to the host machine first, and then shared with the virtual machine using VMware Tools Shared Folders (VMware Tools are discussed in more detail a little later in this chapter.).

■ *Custom.* For more complex network scenarios, you can create a custom connection to map virtual network adapters to specific physical adapters and host-only LAN segments. Each virtual machine by default has a single network adapter labeled Ethernet. You can configure additional network adapters after completing the New Virtual Machine Wizard. Each adapter can use a different type of network connection. The Ethernet adapter, for example, can be bridged while the Ethernet 2 adapter can connect to a host-only network.

I/O Adapter Type

Virtualization products can provide options for different kinds of I/O adapters. Under some circumstances, you may want to use a virtual SCSI adapter instead of a virtual IDE adapter in order to configure a RAID array. VMware provides a virtual ATAPI IDE I/O adapter and allows you to select one of two types of virtual SCSI I/O adapters using the dialog box shown in Figure 2.3. VMware provides multiple SCSI adapter choices. Under VMware, depending on the virtual-machine usage scenario and the guest operating system, the LSI Logic adapter may provide better performance than the default BusLogic adapter depending on the driver implementation in the guest operating system.

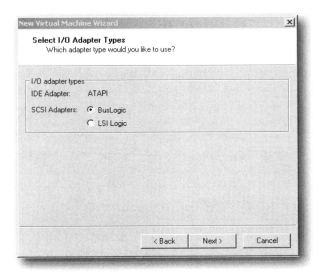

Figure 2.3   Selecting an I/O Adapter

VMware Disks: Virtual and Physical

The ability to use either a physical disk or a virtual disk provides flexible storage options for your virtual machines. In VMware, virtual machines can use both virtual and physical disks. A virtual disk, which stores the contents of the virtual machine's hard disk drive, manifests itself as one or more files on the physical hard drive of the host machine. When using the physical disk option, VMware allows a virtual machine to directly access a physical hard drive. VMware virtual drives manifest themselves on the host machines hard disk as a single file with a *.vmdk extension, as shown in Figure 2.4.

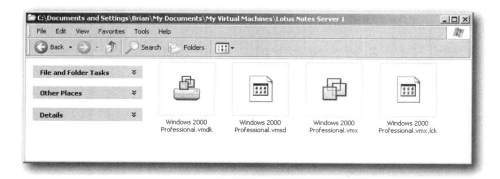

Figure 2.4   Virtual Machine Files

You can copy the virtual disk files manually, but to more easily manage your virtual disk files, use VMware's cloning and snapshot features. Cloning duplicates both the virtual machine and the accompanying virtual machine settings, which VMware stores in separate files. The snapshot feature allows you to save the state of a virtual machine, including the contents of the virtual disks and memory, at a specific point in time, including whether the virtual machine is powered on, powered off, or suspended.

VMware virtual machines can also use physical disks directly, although VMware considers the use of these disks to be an advanced configuration. In some cases, though, the need for high capacity storage will lead you to use a physical disk. VMware 5.5 limits virtual disks to 950 GB, while physical disks can be as large as 2 terabytes (TB). You can also use the physical disk option on a dual-boot system to boot up a second operating system that has been installed natively on the host machine. Be aware that booting up an existing operating system in VMware is analogous to moving that hard drive to a different physical machine; the change from physical hardware to virtual hardware requires different drivers. If you are using a Windows guest operating system, this change from physical to virtual hardware may also interfere with the operating system's activation mechanism. This is due to Windows Activation being based on detecting changes to the underlying hardware. Moving a virtual machine from one piece of physical hardware to another may cause the Activation system to prompt for a product key again and therefore require the use of another unique license. However the use of Volume License Keys (if they are available to your company as they are not to all) can be one way to work around this restriction in a legitimate fashion.

VMware

VMware offers a variety of different virtualization products for workstation and server environments. These products share many of the same features and configuration options. Each version of VMware, with the exception of VMware ESX Server, runs on top of a host operating system such as Microsoft Windows or Linux.

Advanced Memory Configuration

VMware provides options for managing the total physical memory available to all virtual machines. By restricting the amount of memory, you can preserve the performance of other memory-hungry applications running on the host operating system.

Figure 2.5 shows the Preferences dialog box and the options for allocating memory. VMware by default limits the use of the host operating system's virtual memory capabilities to prevent excessive disk swapping. Selecting the option to fit all virtual machine memory into reserved host RAM improves overall performance by preventing any disk swapping at all. Alternatively, the option to allow most virtual machine memory to be swapped provides the most aggressive use of memory and may be necessary if you want to run virtual machines on a host machine with limited physical memory.

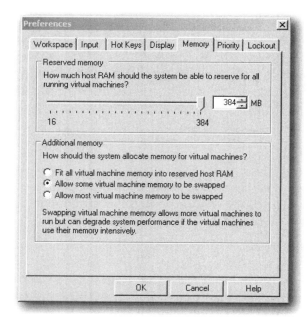

Figure 2.5   Configuring Memory Preferences

Legacy Virtual Disk Support

While you can use a virtual disk from an earlier version of VMware, it cannot take full advantage of all of the features of VMware versions 5.0 and higher. In particular, the snapshot feature is not available, and during a cloning process you cannot use a legacy virtual disk as the original. To take full advantage of these features, use the virtual disk upgrade option shown in Figure 2.6.

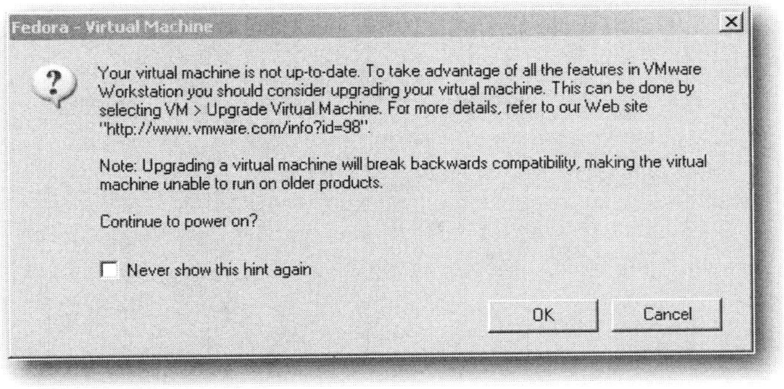

Figure 2.6   Upgrading a Virtual Machine

Teams

The VMware team feature supports the creation of more complex network scenarios. A *team* is a set of virtual machines, which you can power on and manage as a unit and which share one or more virtual LAN segments. You can configure a VMware team to boot the virtual machines in a specific order, preventing unnecessary errors such as those that can occur when a client system finishes the boot process before the server system has started all necessary services.

You might use the team feature to test multi-tier applications or router configurations. Or an administrator might use teams to create a virtual lab for testing, simulating a variety of network structures and conditions, including bandwidth limitations and packet loss. Figure 2.7 shows and example of a VMware team configured with multiple LAN segments of varying speeds.

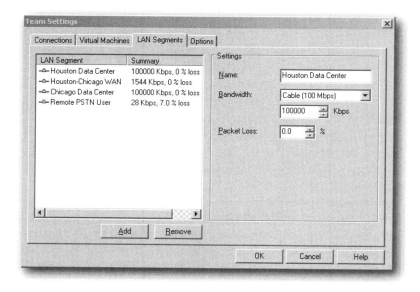

Figure 2.7   VMware Team Settings

Cloning

VMware supports a special mechanism for copying virtual machines called *cloning*. Cloning makes a duplicate virtual machine based on an original parent virtual machine. While you could simply copy the virtual disk files to create copies of a virtual machine, the cloning process copies both these disk files and other important configuration files. The cloning process also makes necessary changes to the copy, such as changing the MAC address of any virtual network adapters. Cloned virtual machines simplify software testing by quickly providing multiple copies of a known, baseline platform. They also speed up and simplify the process of provisioning new virtual machines. VMware supports two types of clones: full and linked.

■ *Full clone.* A full clone duplicates the entire original virtual machine, including any virtual drives. Once VMware creates the clone, the new virtual machine functions independently of the parent. A full clone generally provides better performance than a linked clone, but also takes longer to create and uses significantly more disk space than its linked equivalent.

■ *Linked clone.* A linked clone contains only the differences between the clone and its linked parent virtual machine. Linked clones provide two key benefits: fast installation and efficient use of storage. A linked clone conserves significant disk space because large amounts of data will likely remain the same for both the parent and the clone for the entire lifespan of the virtual machine. The base configuration of the guest operating system itself, for example, will be largely identical on each copy of a virtual. In some scenarios, the use of linked clones can create performance issues, but in many scenarios the performance impact is minimal.

A linked clone cannot operate without its parent, so VMware provides an optional mechanism called *templates* for protecting the parent. Figure 2.8 shows the Virtual Machine Settings dialog box where you can configure a template. VMware does not automatically set the parent machine as a template. A virtual machine template cannot be added to or deleted from a team.

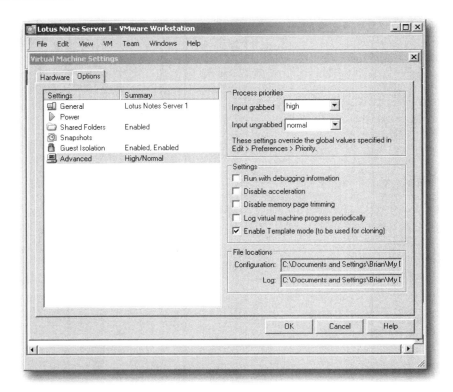

Figure 2.8   Configuring a Template for a Clone

Suppose, for example, that you need to test two Windows XP applications, and you want to run them on separate virtual machines to be certain that the two applications do not interfere with each other and affect the test. Without using linked clones, each virtual machine might require approximately 1.5 GB of physical disk space for the base installation. Using linked clones saves significant disk space because only the parent virtual disk image contains the complete operating system.

The parent virtual machine can include additional applications of your choice. Creating a set of virtual machine templates for common roles, such as workstation, database server, or Web server can result in significant disk savings by avoiding the duplication of both the operating system and applications. Creating a linked clone does not require the copying of the parent virtual machine's entire virtual drive, so creating linked clones will be much faster than creating the same number of full clones.

VMware Tools

The VMware tools package, installed on the virtual machine, provides specialized device drivers to support VMware's virtual hardware and enhanced interface integration between the host and client operating systems.

Tools Driver Support

The default drivers for most guest operating systems provide basic support for essential hardware such as the keyboard, mouse, and VGA adapter. VMware Tools replaces these standard device drivers with drivers that specifically support the virtual hardware. Figure 2.9 shows some of the virtual devices provided by VMware Tools, as shown in Device Manager when using Windows 2000 as the guest operating system, including:

- VMware Virtual S SCSI Device hard disk
- VMware SVGA II display adapter
- VMware Accelerated AMD PCNet[†] Adapter network interface card
- VMware Pointing Device

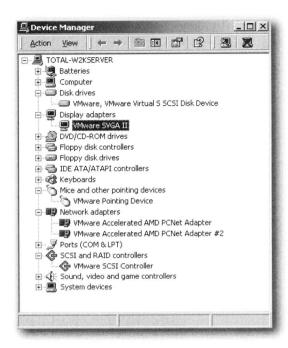

Figure 2.9   Windows 2000 Device Manager Showing the VMware Tools
Virtual Device Drivers

Interface Integration

VMware Tools provides several interface enhancements, including:

■ Improved handling of keyboard and mouse events, including the ability to automatically shift the mouse focus between the virtual and host operating system.

■ Control of some VMware options, such as connecting and disconnecting removable virtual devices from within the virtual operating system interface.

■ Support for shrinking the virtual hard disk file by reclaiming unused virtual disk space, minimizing the size of the virtual disk file on the host machine.

■ Shared folder support.

■ Drag-and-drop support between the virtual machine and the host machine.

Shared Folders

VMware provides a standard method to access shared folders on the host machine from the virtual machines. The folders to be shared are configured for each virtual machine through the VMware console. Once the folders have been configured and VMware Tools has been installed on the virtual machine, you can access the shared folders from the virtual machine using the UNC path \\.host\Shared Folders as shown in Figure 2.10.

Figure 2.10   Accessing Shared Folders from within the Guest Operating System

Snapshots

VMware snapshots save three elements of a virtual machine's state: memory, settings, and disk states. The process of creating a snapshot is similar to simply suspending the machine using the guest operating system's hibernate function. During snapshot creation, VMware creates files on the host machine's physical drive that include the contents of the virtual machine's memory, settings such as the number of network cards and the location of virtual drives, and the actual contents of the virtual disks. VMware can keep multiple snapshots for each virtual machine, allowing the administrator to revert the machine to an earlier state. Figure 2.11 shows the VMware Snapshot Manager, which provides a graphical interface for managing snapshots for each virtual machine.

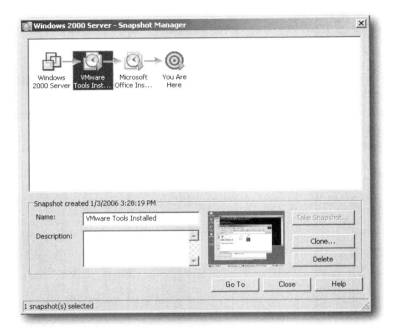

Figure 2.11   VMware Snapshot Manager

VMware Hardware Support

VMware simplifies hardware support by providing a standardized set of virtual devices. VMware maps each virtual device to a specific physical resource on the host machine. The standard devices provided include a keyboard, mouse, memory, sound card, and hard drives. VMware also supports optional devices such as serial, parallel, and USB ports. Support for USB devices remains an area of active development. While VMware already supports the use of USB keyboards and mice, you should test other USB devices on a case-by-case basis to ensure they work properly.

VMware Screen Captures and Video

VMware provides two features, screen captures and video, to help developers and other end users document procedures and events happening within the virtual machine. VMware offers three levels of quality for captured video: low, medium, and best, while offering only a standard-quality bitmap option for screen captures.

Importing Virtual Machines from Other Products

VMware can import Windows 2000, XP, and 2003 server virtual machines from Microsoft Virtual PC, Norton Ghost[†], and Symantec LiveState[†]. You can import the following versions of Symantec LiveState Recovery and Norton Ghost system image files as VMware virtual machines:

- Microsoft Virtual PC, version 7 or later
- Microsoft Virtual Server, all versions
- Symantec LiveState Recovery Desktop, all versions
- Symantec LiveState Recovery Standard Server, all versions
- Symantec LiveState Recovery Advanced Server, all versions
- Norton Ghost, version 9 and later

You cannot import a virtual machine that uses Windows 9x, MS-DOS, or a Linux distribution as its guest operating system.

The VMware Product Line

VMware offers both workstation and server-based products. The Workstation products include:

- VMware Workstation
- VMware Player
- VMware ACE[†]

VMware Server solutions include:

- VMware ESX[†]
- VMware GSX[†]
- VMware VirtualCenter
- VMware P2V Assistant

Workstation Products

VMware Workstation provides a virtualization solution for the individual desktop. Currently in version 5.5, VMware Workstation runs on top of a host operating system. The host operating system can be either Linux or a current version of Microsoft Windows, including Windows Server 2003 x64 Edition with Service Pack 1 and Windows XP Professional x64 Edition with Service Pack 1. Figure 2.12 shows the VMware Workstation console.

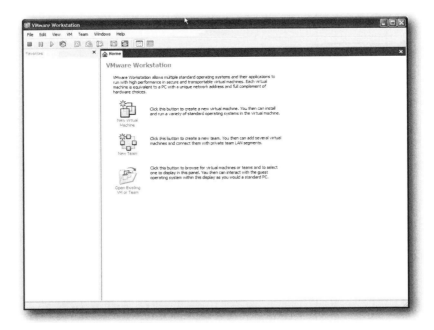

Figure 2.12   The VMware Workstation Console

VMware Workstation supports these guest operating systems:

- Windows Server 2003
- Windows XP
- Windows 2000 Server and Professional
- Windows NT 4.0 Server and Workstation
- Windows ME, Windows 98, and Windows 95
- Windows 3.11 and MS-DOS 6
- Linux distributions such as RedHat, SUSE, TurboLinux, and Mandrake
- FreeBSD

- Novell Netware 6.5, 6.0, 5.1
- Experimental support for Windows Vista and Sun Solaris 9 and 10 for Intel platforms

VMware Player

The free VMware Player enables any user to run most virtual machines created by VMware Workstation, VMware GSX Server, or VMware ESX Server. VMware Player provides a useful and cost-effective way to distribute demos or special purpose virtual machines. VMware, for example, provides a Linux-based browser appliance. Users who want to safeguard their host PC from viruses and spyware can safely surf the Internet using the browser appliance running in the VMware Player. Any Web site viewed using the virtual machine's browser has no access to the host machine, which eliminates many of the risks inherent in browsing the Internet. Figure 2.13 shows the VMware Player running a virtual machine browser.

VMware Player is intended for use with stand-alone virtual machines and cannot run virtual machines that use certain advanced VMware features, including cloning, snapshots, and VMware teams.

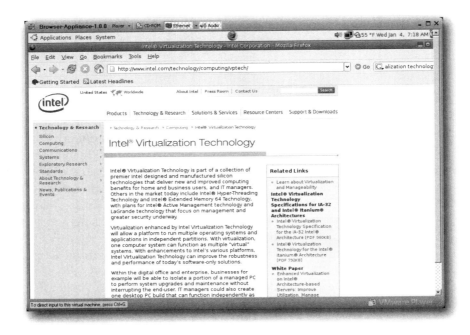

Figure 2.13   A Virtual Machine Running under VMware Player

VMware Assured Computing Environment (ACE)

VMware Assured Computing Environment (ACE) consists of two products: VMware ACE Manager and VMware ACE for end-user PCs. A security administrator can use VMware ACE to create a set of virtual machines for end users. Instead of having to manage the physical PCs, an administrator can distribute a properly configured and secured virtual computing environment to the desktop.

Using VMware ACE Manager, an administrator can create MSI-compatible packages—single-file executables that can install both VMware ACE for end-user PCs and one or more virtual machines. The administrator can use any existing network infrastructure to distribute the MSI packages.

VMware ACE introduces the concept of Virtual Rights Management (VRM) technology. Using VRM, an administrator can apply a variety of restrictions on the VMware ACE virtual machines:

■   Access to the virtual machine

- Times of day when the virtual machine can be used
- Access to network resources from the virtual machine
- Access to hardware on the host PC by the virtual machine
- Copy protection and encryption options for the virtual machine

For example, you can configure a virtual machine to allow VPN access to the corporate network but to disallow use of the USB ports on the host PC, preventing users from copying data directly from the virtual machine to a USB device.

Current versions of VMware ACE require Windows 2000 or later as the host operating system for both VMware ACE Manager and VMware ACE for end-user PCs. Any guest operating system supported by the other VMware products will run with VMware ACE.

VMware GSX Server

VMware GSX Server uses the same technology as VMware Workstation but provides enhancements that support production virtual servers. These enhancements include:

- Option for headless operation—no monitor required
- Web-based management interface
- Support for up to eight CPUs
- Support for up to four virtual machines per CPU

VMware GSX Server installs on top of a host operating system, just like VMware Workstation, and uses the same configuration files and virtual disk formats.

VMware Server (Beta)

Just prior to the printing of this book, VMware released a beta version of VMware Server. VMware Server is the freely available version of GSX server. Final product details are not clear at the present time about the forthcoming release of the GSX product line but the significant point about this release is that it will be completely free in the same manner as the VMware Player.

VMware ESX Server

Intended as a data center solution, VMware ESX Server installs directly on top of the hardware without the need for a host operating system.

VMware ESX Server supports numerous features that support data center needs, including pre-boot execution environment (PXE) support, VMotion[†], and Virtual SMP.

VMware ESX Server PXE support allows you to install an operating system over the network with minimal configuration on the target machine. Commonly used in large networks for installing operating systems on physical machines, the PXE support in VMware ESX Server allows administrators to use their traditional operating system deployment tools when configuring a virtual machine.

VMware Virtual SMP allows virtual machines to access multiple processors. In VMware Workstation or VMware GSX server, each virtual machine can access only a single physical processor on the host machine. Virtual SMP eliminates this barrier and allows virtual machines to fully support SMP-enabled applications running on the virtual machines. Virtual SMP is available as an add-on to VMware ESX Server and is not included in the standard VMware ESX Server license.

Using VMotion technology, VMware ESX server can move a virtual machine that is powered on and running from one physical host machine to another without having to first shut it down. This allows administrators to perform hardware maintenance and deal with hardware failures without interrupting service availability. VMotion requires that the host machines be connected to the same storage area network (SAN).

Other data-center enabling features of VMware ESX server include:

■ Support for up to 80 concurrent virtual machines using up to 64 GB of RAM on a 16 CPU system

■ Resource access guarantees for CPU, RAM, network bandwidth and disk I/O

■ Systems management integration with popular systems management products

■ API and scripting for controlling virtual machines

■ Clustering support

VMware ESX server uses its own file format for virtual disks. Virtual disks imported from other versions of VMware, including Workstation and GSX Server, must be converted to the VMware ESX virtual disk format before they can be used with VMware ESX Server.

ESX and GSX Server Comparison

Table 2.1 outlines the key differences between the VMware GSX and ESX Servers.

Table 2.1   ESX and GSX Server Comparison

Feature	ESX	GSX
Typical system	2–8 CPU	2–16 CPU
Virtual SMP support	Yes	No
Host operating system	Installs directly on top of hardware	Installs on Linux or Windows Server 2003
Typical usages	Multi-tier applications, servers, in-house applications	Application servers, utility applications
System RAM	Up to 64 GB	Up to 64 GB
VLAN Support	Yes	No
Resource controls	Dynamic memory, CPU, disk and network	Static memory configuration

VMware P2V Assistant

The VMware P2V Assistant transforms physical PCs into equivalent virtual machines. The process resembles creating a backup image of a physical machine and restoring the image to a new machine with different hardware.

The process involves using the P2V Assistant Boot CD to boot the existing physical PC. The source PC then attempts to contact a helper machine running the P2V Assistant. Finally, the P2V Assistant creates the virtual disk and configuration files for the new virtual machine on the helper machine.

The VMware P2V Assistant automates parts of the process of migrating existing physical PCs to new virtual PCs; but additional tools, such as Microsoft's sysprep tool, may be required to finish the migration process.

VMware Virtual Center

VMware Virtual Center provides an interface for managing large virtual infrastructures. With VMware Virtual Center, you can monitor, manage and maintain hundreds of servers from a single console. Typical tasks might include provisioning new servers, monitoring system availability, and moving workloads between physical servers.

Microsoft

Microsoft offers two virtualization products that share much of the same underlying technology. Microsoft Virtual PC competes as a desktop-based virtualization solution, suitable for developers and end users. Microsoft Virtual Server provides solutions for servers and data centers. Both products share the same virtual hard drive format and virtual machine configuration file format, although some changes to the configuration files may be necessary when running a virtual machine created using Microsoft Virtual PC under Microsoft Virtual Server. The user interface for each product, however, differs greatly.

Microsoft Virtual PC

Microsoft Virtual PC uses a simple graphical console application, shown in Figure 2.14, for managing virtual machines. This console offers relatively few configuration options compared to Microsoft Virtual Server's Web-based interface.

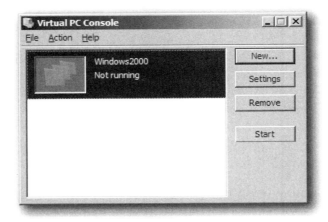

Figure 2.14   Microsoft Virtual PC Console

With Microsoft Virtual PC, each running guest operating system displays in its own window as a native Windows application, as shown in Figure 2.15. A set of menus control access to virtual machine settings and various actions, including options for powering the virtual machine on and off and connecting the virtual CD drive to specific drives or disk images on the host machine.

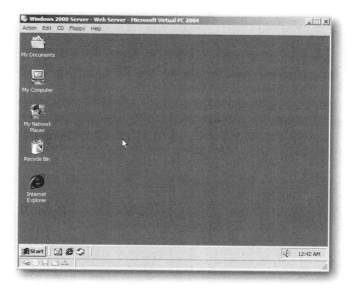

Figure 2.15   Microsoft Virtual PC Guest Operating System

Supported Host Operating Systems

Microsoft Virtual PC requires one of these host operating systems:

- Windows XP Professional
- Windows XP Tablet Edition
- Windows 2000 Professional

Supported Guest Operating Systems

Microsoft Virtual PC supports these guest operating systems:

- Windows XP (all versions)

- Windows 2000 Professional
- Windows NT 4.0 (SP6A required)
- Windows ME
- Windows 98
- Windows 95
- MS DOS 6.22
- Windows 3.11
- OS/2 Warp 4

Creating a Virtual Machine

The New Virtual Machine Wizard, shown in Figure 2.16, allows you to create a new virtual machine under Microsoft Virtual PC. The wizard creates a standard virtual machine platform with a typical selection of virtual hardware. Microsoft Virtual PC offers a more limited set of virtual machine options than Microsoft Virtual Server. For example, Microsoft Virtual PC offers no support for adding a virtual SCSI host adapter or for clustering.

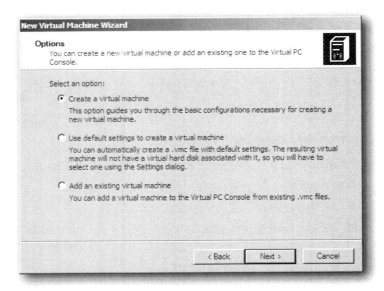

Figure 2.16 Creating a Virtual Machine under Microsoft Virtual PC

Microsoft Virtual Server

Microsoft Virtual Server does not provide a console-based control or configuration applications. Instead, the Web-based interface shown in Figure 2.17 controls, configures, and manages Microsoft Virtual Server's virtual machines. Using an ActiveX[†] control, even the graphical user interface of a running virtual machine manifests itself in a browser window. The use of the Web-based interface facilitates remote access and headless operation. Once the Microsoft Virtual Server host machines have been installed, you can perform all management tasks from a single client system running Internet Explorer 5.5 or later.

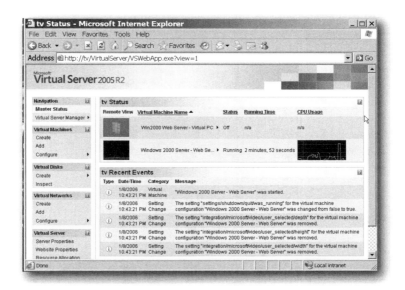

Figure 2.17   Virtual Server 2005 R2 Console

Microsoft Virtual Machine Remote Control Server

Under normal operations, machines running under Microsoft Virtual Server do not appear in their own application window. Instead, a thumbnail image of the virtual machines user interface appears in the management Web page. To interact with the virtual machine, Microsoft Virtual Server uses a browser-based application that connects to the Virtual Machine Remote Control (VMRC) server, as shown in Figure 2.18.

The first time the browser connects to the VMRC server, the browser downloads an ActiveX control. This acts as the VMRC client, displaying the virtual machine's user interface in the browser window. The VMRC client application uses TCP/IP port 5900 to connect to the VMRC server, so any firewalls between the client machine and the server must be configured to allow connections on that port. The VMRC client uses the same TCP/IP port as VNC, a widely-used remote control application. However, the VMRC client uses proprietary Microsoft authentication protocols and is no longer compatible with the standard VNC client. The use of VMRC instead of a console application integrates the client with the other Web-based management utilities and facilitates the headless use of Microsoft Virtual Server in the data center. Optional SSL encryption support is available for security purposes.

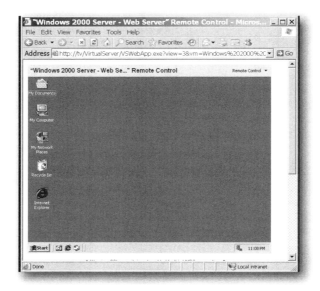

Figure 2.18   Using the VMRC Client to Access a Guest Operating System

Supported Host Operating Systems

Microsoft Virtual Server requires one of these host operating systems:

■ Microsoft Windows Server 2003 Standard Edition, Enterprise Edition, or Datacenter Edition or later

- Windows Server 2003 Standard x64 Edition, Enterprise x64 Edition, Datacenter x64 Edition or later versions
- Windows Small Business Server 2003 Standard Edition or Premium Edition
- Windows XP Professional Service Pack 2 or later (for non-production use only).

Supported Guest Operating Systems

Microsoft Virtual Server supports these guest operating systems:

- Windows XP (all versions)
- Windows 2000 Professional
- Windows NT 4.0 (SP6A required)
- Windows ME
- Windows 98
- Windows 95
- MS-DOS 6.22
- Windows 3.11
- OS/2 Warp 4

You can use other operating systems, such as Windows Vista, as well as non-Microsoft operating systems, such as Linux, as guest operating systems, but they are not officially supported by Microsoft at this time.

Creating Virtual Machines with Microsoft Virtual Server

Microsoft Virtual Server's browser-based configuration utility, shown in Figure 2.19, provides a fuller set of options for configuring virtual machines than the basic interface that Microsoft Virtual PC offers. Microsoft Virtual Server provides options for advanced hardware configurations, including SCSI adapters, complex virtual network infrastructures, and iSCSI support for creating clusters.

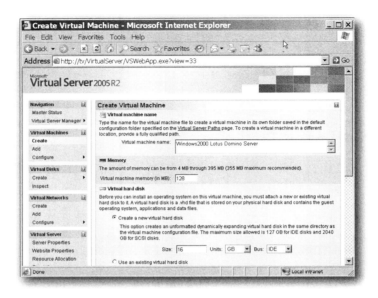

Figure 2.19   Web Interface for Creating a New Virtual Machine under Microsoft Virtual Server

Additional Virtual Server Features

Here are some additional features that Microsoft Virtual Server offers:

- Scripting support
- Compatibility with Windows Server System products, including Automated Deployment Service, Systems Management Server 2003, and Microsoft Operations Management 2005
- Delegated management using standard Windows user accounts
- Multiprocessor support, but only one processor for each virtual machine
- Support for x64 hosts
- PXE booting from the emulated network card

Virtual Disks for Microsoft Virtual PC and Virtual Server

Microsoft Virtual PC and Server share the same virtual disk format, supporting the four types of virtual disks shown in the dialog box in Figure 2.20.

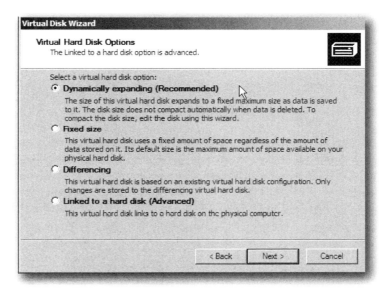

Figure 2.20   Hard Disk Options for Microsoft Virtual PC and Virtual Server

- *Dynamically expanding.* This type of disk appears as a single file with a *.vhd extension on the host machine's hard drive. While the guest operating system sees the drive size as the full-size, maximum disk size specified, the virtual disk file starts as a small 3 KB file and expands, as needed, up to the maximum specified when creating the virtual disk. Dynamically-expanding disks use the host machine's storage more efficiently, although the disk expansion process can have a negative impact on performance.

- *Fixed-size.* Creating a fixed-size disk avoids the performance issue of a dynamically-expanding drive. If you specify a fixed-size disk, a file with that capacity is created on the host machine's hard drive. In addition to the performance benefits, using fixed-sized disks ensures that the disk space will be available on the host machine when needed. You can select the fixed-size disk option when you create the virtual machine, or you can, if necessary, convert an existing dynamically-expanding disk to a fixed-size disk.

■ *Differencing virtual.* To use physical disk space more efficiently, Microsoft Virtual PC offers the option to create differencing disks. Conceptually similar to the linked-clone option that VMware offers, a differencing disk contains only the differences between the new virtual disk, called the child, and the original virtual disk, called the parent. The differencing virtual disk file starts off small and expands as needed, similar to the dynamically-expanding disk. Microsoft recommends write-protecting the parent virtual disk to prevent its being modified by other processes. If the parent virtual disk becomes damaged, all child differencing disks based on that parent will be unusable.

■ *Linked virtual.* A linked virtual hard disk is one that is linked to a physical hard disk. A linked virtual disk provides a way to convert an entire physical hard disk into a virtual disk. A linked disk should never be used as the boot disk for a virtual machine.

Undo Disks

Both Microsoft Virtual PC and Microsoft Virtual Server support *undo disks*. With this option enabled, any changes made to the disk are stored in a temporary file and the virtual disk file itself is not altered by the virtual machine. When the virtual machine shuts down, the changes are discarded and the virtual machine reverts to its previous configuration. Undo disks help to provide a stable, known configuration for testing purposes. In this way, they are conceptually similar to the Snapshot functionality in VMware products.

Figure 2.21 shows the configuration interface for configuring undo disks.

Figure 2.21   Microsoft Virtual Server's Undo Disk Configuration

Virtual Machine Additions

Microsoft provides Virtual Machine Additions, which improve the integration of the host and guest operating systems. These applications, installed on each guest operating system, allow the Microsoft Virtual PC and Microsoft Virtual Server management utilities to interact with the guest operating system. With Virtual Machine Additions installed, for example, the virtual machine management utilities can shut down the guest operating system directly. Microsoft Virtual PC supports additional enhancements that are not available using Microsoft Virtual Server's VMRC client, including drag-and-drop support between the guest and host operating systems.

Virtual Server 2005 Migration Toolkit (VSMT)

Microsoft provides the Virtual Server 2005 Migration Toolkit (VSMT) to assist in migrating from physical to virtual machines. VSMT is not a stand-alone product and requires both Microsoft Virtual Server and Automated Deployment Services (ADS) 1.0.

Hardware Support

Microsoft Virtual PC and Microsoft Virtual Server emulate a basic set of virtual hardware, including:

- S3 Trio Video Card

- Intel / DEC 21140 network card
- Sound Blaster[†] 16 ISA sound card (Microsoft Virtual PC only)
- Intel 440BX motherboard chipset

Microsoft Virtual Server and Microsoft Virtual PC currently do not support USB devices other than keyboards and a single mouse. Also, sound support is available only for Microsoft Virtual PC.

Xen

Xen, an open-source project hosted by the University of Cambridge Computer Laboratory, provides a paravirtualization-based virtualization solution. Unlike the Microsoft and VMware virtualization products, which run unmodified operating systems using full virtualization, the paravirtualization approach requires modifications to the guest operating system. Until recently, those required modifications limited Xen to using open-source guest operating systems. Combining Xen with Intel® Virtualization Technology, however, opens up the possibility of running unmodified operating systems with Xen.

Xen Hypervisor and Xen Domains

The Xen Hypervisor, also known as the virtual machine monitor, sits between the hardware and the guest operating systems and manages the use of system resources. Unlike VMware or Virtual PC, Xen has no true host operating system. Instead, the first virtual machine provides an interface to the hypervisor for configuring virtual machines and managing systems resources.

Domain 0: The First Virtual Machine

Xen refers to each virtual machine as a domain. The first domain, called Domain 0 or Dom0, runs a modified version of Linux and provides access to the hypervisor using the xend daemon. A daemon in Linux is roughly equivalent to a service on a Windows-based system.

Commands issued to the xend daemon are passed to the hypervisor, which controls and manages access to the host machine's resources. Instead of providing a single graphical management interface on the Domain 0 virtual machine, management tasks are performed using command line tools such as xm. xm is the primary tool for issuing commands to the hypervisor.

Domain U: Additional Virtual Machines

Each additional domain is given an identifying domain name. These additional domains are sometimes referred to generically as "Domain U" or "DomU," as in "CentOS is supported as a DomU operating system."

Note | Don't confuse a Xen domain with other uses of the term *domain*. A domain in Xen is a virtual machine, and a Xen domain name is simply the name used to refer to the virtual machine when using management tools such as xm.

Managing the Process of Image Creation, Migration, and Deletion

The xend daemon manages the tasks of creating, deleting, migrating, and assigning resources to each domain. The xm command provides the primary interface for sending instructions from Domain 0's console to the xend daemon. For example, the command to create a new virtual machine domain looks like this:

```
#xm create -c ~/new_vm_template.conf name=virutal_server1
```

The text file new_vm_template.conf contains the configuration options for the new virtual machine, including the location of the virtual disk file and the amount of memory to assign to the virtual machine.

For more information about options for using xm, type:

```
#xm help
```

Xen includes a few additional console tools such as xencons, which open a terminal session on a virtual machine, and xentop, shown in Figure 2.22, which displays the status of currently running virtual machines.

Figure 2.22   The xentop Tool Displays the Status of Each Running Virtual Machine

The use of the xm command for configuration tasks makes scripting Xen management tasks relatively simple. The implementation on the Xen Demo CD, for example, includes desktop shortcuts for launching scripts that create new Debian and CentOS virtual machines from a template, as shown in Figure 2.23.

Figure 2.23   Creating a New Virtual Machine When Using the Xen Demo CD

A Web-based interface for managing Xen, called xensv, is currently under development, but at this time the xm command remains the only tool for accomplishing many management tasks with Xen.

Connecting to a virtual machine GUI using VNC

Users often require access to the graphical user interface of the virtual machine. Although not technically part of Xen itself, the typical solution for enabling access to the GUI is to install a VNC server on the virtual machine. Accessing the virtual machine GUI using VNC looks very similar to the mechanism that Microsoft Virtual Server uses for GUI access, except that you can use any standard VNC viewer application. Because standard VNC does not include authentication or encryption, administrators need to take extra steps to secure these VNC connections by tunneling them over a VPN or SSH connection. Figure 2.24 shows the VNC client connecting to a Xen virtual machine.

Figure 2.24   Xen Virtual Machine, Viewed Using the VNC Client

Supported Operating Systems for Xen 3.0

Xen 3.0 currently requires Linux running kernel 2.6 for both the Domain 0 operating system and the Domain U (guest) operating systems. Support for other operating systems, both modified and unmodified, remains under development.

Modified Operating Systems

To take full advantage of the performance benefits of paravirtualization, most guest operating systems running under Xen will continue to require some modification. In addition to the currently support Linux with kernel 2.6, development continues on support for:

- FreeBSD 5.3
- NetBSD 2.0
- Plan 9
- ReactOS

Unmodified Operating Systems and Intel Virtualization Technology

With the introduction of Intel Virtualization Technology, Xen can now support unmodified guest operating systems. While open-source guest operating systems such as Linux will likely continue to include some level of modification to maximize performance, the ability to run unmodified operating systems opens up the possibility of running Windows as a guest operating system in production environments.

Disk in Xen: Virtual Block Devices (VBDs)

Xen refers to virtual disks as Virtual Block Devices (VBDs). In standard Linux terminology, a block device is any device whose data can be accessed in blocks and that provides random access. This definition includes hard drives, removable media drives, and network shares. From the perspective of the virtual machine, all VBDs look like a standard mass storage device, but Xen allows the VBDs to refer to any block device that the Domain 0 operating system can access. In practice, VBDs generally map to one of the following:

- an individual virtual disk file
- a physical disk partition
- a Logical Volume Management (LVM) volume
- a Network File System (NFS) share

With Xen, the virtual-disk file option works in much the same way that virtual disks work in Microsoft Virtual PC or VMware. Unlike VMware or Microsoft Virtual PC, however, Xen does not implement a specific file format for virtual disk files. Instead, Xen allows the guest operating system to simply read and write data directly to the file in much the same way that a Linux machine would access a mounted disk image. Because of the technique used by Domain 0 to access the virtual disk file, virtual disks do not perform well when used for I/O intensive tasks.

Note

> When running I/O-intensive applications or servers on a virtual machine, avoid using file-backed VBDs.

Using a physical disk as a VBD avoids the performance problems associated with a file-backed VBD. The physical disk can be any type of physical disk recognized by the Domain 0 operating system and can include Storage Area Networks (SANs) as well as more traditional disk technologies such as IDE and SCSI.

Logical Volume Management (LVM) provides a more flexible solution, allowing multiple physical devices to be treated as a single block device. LVM-backed VBDs are an ideal choice for environments where the storage requirements of the virtual machines change over time. LVM allows an administrator to easily add capacity to an existing volume or to resize disk partitions to meet these changing needs. Combining LVM with a SAN can provide a powerful and flexible storage solution for the data center.

Network File System (NFS) allows Xen to treat an NFS share as a VBD. Using NFS-backed VBDs allows an administrator to take advantage of an existing network infrastructure, but NFS does not always perform well under high loads.

Xen Networking

Xen takes a unique approach to networking. Instead of providing the option of mapping a virtual network interface to either a physical adapter or a host-only virtual adapter, each domain is provided with a point-to-point link to Domain 0. Each virtual machine has a direct connection to the Domain 0 virtual machine, just as if they are two physical machines connected with a crossover cable. Unlike VMware or Microsoft Virtual PC, Xen does not create virtual network segments. Instead, Domain 0 handles all traffic management using the standard Linux tools for routing and bridging network traffic. Many configurations, for example, use iptables to provide network address translation between the virtual machines and the physical network.

Migration: Regular and Live

Xen supports two mechanisms for moving virtual machines between host servers: regular migration and live migration.

Regular Migration

In a regular migration, the guest operating system is suspended by copying the contents of its memory to a file on Domain 0's physical disk. The migration process moves this memory file to the new host server and then restarts the virtual machine. For the new server to properly restart the virtual machine, the server must have access to any VBDs used by the virtual machine. These VBDs must either be moved to the new server or made available by some other means such as a SAN. Because of the time involved in copying the memory file, regular migrations can involve significant down time. The command to perform a regular migration is:

```
# xm migrate source_domain destination_server
```

In this example, source_domain is the Xen domain name for the virtual machine, while destination_server is either the IP address or the Fully Qualified Domain Name (FQDN) of the destination server.

Live Migration

Xen's live migration feature allows the movement of a virtual machine between servers without any service interruption. The virtual machine continues to run on its original host server until the new server finishes booting its copy of the virtual machine. Any existing network connections are maintained, so end users do not notice any disruption of network services. The command for performing a live migration is:

```
# xm migrate --live source_domain destination_server
```

A live migration cannot be done unless two requirements are met:

1. The source and destinations servers must be on the same layer 2 network. Xen migrations cannot take place across a router because moving to a new layer 2 network requires a change to the virtual machine's IP address.

2. The live migration process assumes that any required VBDs will be available, most likely by using a SAN.

Monitoring Server Health

Xen does not provide a way to monitor hardware failures or performance problems, but you can combine third-party monitoring tools with scripted migration commands to create a more robust virtual infrastructure.

Conclusion

VMware, Microsoft, and Xen all provide mature, full-featured virtualization solutions capable of bringing the benefits of virtualization to both the workstation and the data center. This chapter has focused on the features and functionality of these products, providing a high-level overview of the similarities and differences you can expect to see between them. Subsequent chapters delve into use cases for these technologies, their existing limitations, and possibilities for their future use.

Chapter 3

Impact of Virtualization

> *Some day, on the corporate balance sheet, there will be an entry which reads, "Information"; for in most cases, the information is more valuable than the hardware which processes it.*
>
> —Grace Murray Hopper

Server consolidation has been the "killer usage" for virtualization, and its benefits are well understood. However, many other uses for virtualization are not as obvious or as well known, but are just as significant. Subsequent chapters describe these usages, showing how pervasive virtualization will soon become. However, before listing the usages, it is helpful to consider few fundamental questions. For example, what *really* changes with virtualization and what effect does it have on current usage scenarios? In particular, how does virtualization affect basic requirements, such as availability, reliability, security, and performance, and what are the essential qualities of virtualization that enable the new usage models?

The "Soft" Characteristics of a Virtual Machine

A virtual machine host can be a software-only implementation or it can be implemented to take advantage of the hardware support for virtualization provided Intel® Virtualization Technology (Intel® VT). The virtual machines themselves, however, are simply files stored on a disk that are loaded and run by the virtual machine host, much like a software program running on an operating system today. For example, you can save an entire machine image, from hardware to applications, as a sequence of bits on a disk and send it to someone else. Or, you can dispose of an entire system, from (virtual) hardware to applications, by simply deleting a file. Like software, you can move, delete, copy, version, archive, download, or transmit a virtual machine over a network. Need to archive a previous version of a machine? Simply burn a DVD image and put it on the shelf to be used when needed at a later date. Want to make sure everyone on your software development team is using the same version of hardware and software? Create one standard virtual machine image and distribute copies to the developers.

The conceptually simple act of creating a virtual platform on which we can run many virtual machines causes us to rethink many things that we previously took for granted. It's as if gravity on Earth were suddenly cut in half: cars, airplanes, trains, rockets—they would all have to be redesigned to account for the changes. Similarly with virtualization, the forces at work in the IT world have changed and will cause us to rethink much of what has come before.

Impact of Virtualization on Requirements

One way to analyze the changes brought about by virtualization is to examine the effect virtualization has on the qualities of a solution. If you're involved in specifying product requirements, you're probably familiar with nonfunctional requirements, such as performance, stability, reliability, usability, and so on. These qualities can be hard to quantify and often conflict, requiring tradeoffs to reach an acceptable, balanced solution. For example, a data center might be required to maintain 99.99 percent uptime for servers, yet still be expected to immediately apply security patches as soon as they are available. The data center manager uses available tools and technologies to achieve an acceptable balance among the requirements. Virtualization has now appeared as a mainstream IT technology and changes the dynamics among the requirements—as if gravity were suddenly halved—upsetting the balance that previously existed among them.

The new usages for virtualization discussed in later chapters were developed by considering how virtualization changes current usage models. Therefore, a good starting point to understand the usages and the implications of virtualization changes qualities important to the usage models such as scalability, robustness, reliability, and security.

Scalability

A common requirement is the ability to smoothly adapt to changes in demand for a service. In a data center, scalability is often achieved by deploying more physical hardware to meet demand. This may entail acquiring new machines or having them available and ready to go when needed, which can be expensive to maintain. With virtualization, an organization can have finer-grained control over the scalability of services it provides. For example, consider the case where demand for a particular machine configuration changes over time. An organization, running a mixture of Linux and Microsoft servers, experiences an increase in demand for a service that requires a LAMP (Linux, Apache, MySQL[†], and PHP) configuration. With virtualization it's easy to rebalance the allocation of virtual machines to the available hardware resources, as Figure 3.1 shows. Additional virtual machines can be prepared in advance and quickly deployed as demand increases. To achieve this same level of readiness with a physical solution would mean preparing many hardware systems and keeping them in reserve until they are needed. Figure 3.1 illustrates how a prepared virtual machine (labeled VM A, VM B, and VM C) is deployed to a virtualization platform (labeled VM Host) to meet additional demand for that service.

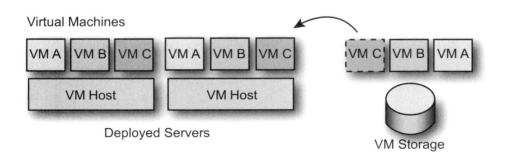

Figure 3.1   Balancing Services to Meet Demand

Virtualization can also help an organization use a "copy exactly" strategy to scale its services. Over time, an organization deploys different hardware that likely is not identical to the previously deployed hardware. However, you can deploy virtual machines that are the same, allowing a server farm of heterogeneous systems to host a group of identical virtual machines, saving time on configuration and testing.

Scalability doesn't just apply to the data center. For example, virtualization can simplify the distribution of an approved machine image to many users. Consider a company that has to roll out an IT-approved version of an operating system and applications to its staff. Many people in the company use notebook computers and access the corporate network using VPN software. The IT department tests the operating system, patches, and VPN software, and approves it for release. The IT department wants this configuration on everyone's computer as soon as possible, with minimal support issues. With a physical machine strategy, the IT department will require everyone to apply operating system patches and to install the approved version of the VPN software. As the organization grows, the support burden will also increase as more and more users encounter installation and upgrade problems.

With a virtual machine strategy, the company can configure and test a single virtual machine image and then distribute that image to everyone. The staff is up and running quickly on the new image with fewer installation hassles, and this method scales easily as the organization grows.

Virtualization enhances scalability because it decouples the underlying physical hardware from the virtual machine image. Operating systems are no longer directly tied to the physical resources underneath. This quality of being able to more quickly and easily scale in a virtualized environment forms the basis for numerous usage models that involve distribution and deployment.

Robustness and Reliability

At the level of an individual program, virtualization does not inherently increase or reduce robustness; an application or device driver with a defect that will likely cause failure on physical hardware will also fail on virtual hardware. However, it will probably be easier and faster to recover and restart a virtual machine than a physical machine. Figure 3.2 shows that it is possible to use virtualization to improve overall system reliability by isolating potentially misbehaving software into a separate partition, shielding the rest of the system from its effects and minimizing the overall impact due to a software failure.

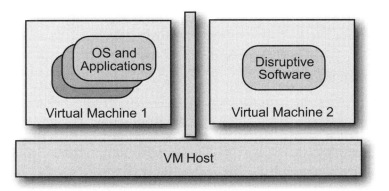

Figure 3.2   Isolating a Service to Improve Overall Stability

However, it is much more expensive to do the same thing with physical hardware. Instead of partitioning the misbehaving software to a separate virtual machine, a dedicated physical machine must be deployed.

If stability, robustness, and reliability are important requirements for your scenarios, virtualization can be put to good use. Also, many usage models can be developed that take advantage of the fact that virtual machines are potentially less expensive to deploy than their physical counterparts.

Security

Another way to take advantage of the isolation that virtual machines provide is to improve security, especially on client machines. Computers, being physically separate, cannot directly interfere with each other except over the network. In the same way, virtual machines on a single host are isolated from each other using virtualization's hardware mechanisms. You can leverage this feature to create dedicated virtual machines to support uses that could potentially be a security risk. For example, when using browsers to surf the Web, users are often tricked into downloading malware, such as spyware or viruses. With virtualization, it is easy to have a partition dedicated to Web browsing. Malware downloaded to this partition is contained and cannot spread to other virtual machines. You can periodically dispose of and refresh the browsing partition with a new, known-to-be-clean partition.

Performance

Virtualization solutions come at a price. Software-based virtualization introduces a layer between the operating system and the physical machine, inherently decreasing performance. Intel Virtualization Technology provides a *hardware-based* solution to virtualization, which makes it possible to minimize the layer between the operating system and the physical hardware, narrowing the performance gap. With the continuation of exponentially increasing trends in computing power, storage, communications bandwidth, and so on, virtualization-enabled computers will be able to host more and more virtual machines, each with adequate processing power, storage capacity, and networking bandwidth to handle tasks at reasonable performance levels.

Availability

Many scenarios require computing systems to have high availability, such as maintaining a server that provides critical business data. A high level of availability is often achieved by using strategies such as replication and redundancy; one system can fail, but there are backup systems ready to come online immediately. Virtualization can enhance these strategies. It is easy to replicate an entire virtual machine image in order to run redundant servers or maintain backups. For example, consider a situation where a hardware failure due to bad disk sectors is imminent on a platform or a network adapter is failing. With a product such as VMware

VMotion an administrator can dynamically move a virtual machine, on the fly, to another hardware platform before the failure interrupts service. The service continues, uninterrupted for its users.

The data itself must also be safeguarded. Backing up data periodically ensures that information is protected from hardware failure, data corruption, fire, and so on and continues to be available to the organization. If a failure occurs, users typically experience a delay as administrators prepare a new server and recover the data. With virtualization, the administrator can create a snapshot of an entire virtual machine instead of just the data. Then, if a catastrophic failure occurs, the backup can be immediately deployed to any virtual machine host, minimizing down time.

Qualities of Virtualization

Understanding the impact of virtualization on the more traditional requirements such as security and availability is one way to look at virtualization. However, a more direct way to understand virtualization is to consider the qualities of virtualization itself and the kinds of usage scenarios that they enable. In other words, using virtualization, what can we now do that wasn't possible before? The following sections list these qualities along with categories of usages that they enable.

Hostability

Virtualization allows a single computer system to host *multiple* virtual machines simultaneously and to control various aspects of each virtual machine, including its hardware configuration, networking capabilities, and so on. These qualities enable the following kinds of usage scenarios:

■ *Resource Utilization Scenarios.* Virtualization enables the consolidation of hardware and a resulting increase in utilization rates. The canonical example is a server environment providing the same level of service with less hardware while realizing hardware and energy savings. Other examples include a testing lab that requires less hardware because of the ability to use virtual machines, or delivering a demonstration of a networked software application on a single hardware platform using virtual machines instead of using many physical platforms.

■ *Networked Application Scenarios.* Virtualization allows many virtual machines to run together on a single physical box, simplifying deployment. Example scenarios in this category include software developers developing and testing networked applications on a single platform, or creating complex multi-machine demo scenarios on a single demo machine.

■ *VM Control Scenarios.* VMM software provides the ability to control various parameters of the virtual machine, such as memory, CPU, networking characteristics, and so on. This facilitates the creation of many virtual hardware platforms for testing.

Platform Independence

The virtual hardware and operating system can vary for each hosted virtual machine. Therefore, with virtualization, it will no longer be necessary to run a single operating system; users have the freedom to select the best operating system for a particular task. The same holds true for applications. Applications are often implemented for a single operating system, such as Microsoft Windows, because of ubiquity on home desktops. However, virtualization offers a choice of operating system for applications. With virtualization, developers can create finely tuned, specialized applications and operating systems on the PC. The dedicated application stack, including operating system, can be delivered as virtual machines.

■ *Legacy Hardware Scenarios.* Because users can specify the virtual hardware in a VM and install older operating systems, they can create VMs that reflect legacy production systems. This allows an organization to maintain support for older legacy systems while upgrading to new hardware and operating systems. This eases the transition to new platforms and saves on hardware costs for what would otherwise be separate systems.

■ *Software Appliance Scenarios.* With virtualization, the entire software stack, from operating system to applications, can be delivered as a whole. These "software appliances" can be created once and used many times, saving the time and expense of duplicating the configuration. For example, a software vendor could deliver pre-release software to customers for testing in a VM. The customer would not have to worry about setup or configuration problems, but could start to use the software immediately.

■ *Specialization Scenarios.* Software appliances can be highly specialized virtual machines, dedicated to a specific purpose. Specialized VMs can also be used to enhance performance, security, and reliability by using simplified, tailored configurations.

■ *Cross-Platform Scenarios.* Because multiple operating systems can run on a single desktop, there are many cross-platform development scenarios possible. For example, a software developer can target multiple operating systems without having to have physical hardware for each target. Similarly, a software testing lab could have a version of every supported operating system and Web browser without dedicating a physical hardware platform to each combination.

Portability

As software, virtual machines are inherently more portable than their physical counterparts. Virtual machines can be moved automatically between physical host machines or can be transported manually for use on different machines. This portability forms the basis of many new usage models.

■ *Relocation and Failover Scenarios.* Some virtualization software allows an administrator to move a virtual machine between host platforms. Administrators can use this capability to move VMs off of failing platforms onto other, stable platforms, maximizing uptime experienced by users.

■ *Portable Virtual Machine Scenarios.* The portability of virtual machines simplifies the task of working on the same project from multiple locations. For example, users can bring their virtual machines with them, complete with applications, data, and configuration, and then use the computing resources available to them to run their virtual machines. Portable VMs also enable people to create complex configurations in advance and use them later, such as when creating demonstrations involving multiple platforms or when preparing an environment for training.

Isolation

Virtual machines are isolated from each other by hardware protection mechanisms built into the platform. The separation of virtual machines, where one virtual machine cannot disrupt or directly access the others, enables many security and robustness scenarios.

- *Isolation and Quarantine Scenarios.* In this category, a virtual machine is isolated for security purposes. For example, a user can browse the Web using a special virtual machine dedicated to this task, keeping the primary desktop system free of viruses and spyware. Or, a virtual machine that has been compromised can have its network access disabled, limiting the spread of viruses throughout the network.

- *Robustness Scenarios.* Software that has occasional stability problems that disrupt the rest of the system can be isolated into its own virtual machine, increasing overall robustness and availability.

- *Exclusive Access and Control Scenarios.* In some situations it is convenient to grant complete control of a virtual machine to another entity, such as a service provider, instead of using a physically separate platform. This reduces the amount of hardware required while maintaining the degree of control required by the external entity.

Duplicability

Virtual machines can be easily duplicated; the bits are simply copied from one location to another. This ability to generate one or more duplicates of a single virtual machine snapshot, frozen at a point in time, is the key element in many usages discussed in this book and for many not yet imagined. Here are a few categories where this quality comes into play:

- *Snapshot Scenarios.* A snapshot of the current state of a virtual machine is analogous to a file copy operation and can be used in similar ways, such as save known good images, to archive or backup particular version, or to serve as a branch for further changes.

- *Standardized Baseline Scenarios.* Often, many people need to use exactly the same operating system and applications. With virtualization, you can create a standard image and share it with others.

■ *Communication Scenarios.* Many scenarios can be enhanced by the ability to communicate the exact state of the system to someone else. For example, using virtualization, a tester can take a snapshot of a virtual machine at the time of a failure and provide this to the developer instead of requiring the developer to spend time recreating the environment under which the failure occurred. The developer can then run the virtual machine directly instead of spending time duplicating the environment.

■ *Testing Scenarios.* Software testers can also prepare many different virtual machines to test different target environments. Virtual machine images can support testing matrices that contain different operating system versions, different Web browsers, and so on.

Persistence

Virtual machines can be stored for future use and restarted when needed.

■ *Backup Scenarios.* You can save a virtual machine snapshot in case a hardware or software failure or natural disaster causes data loss.

■ *Archiving Scenarios.* You can save a virtual machine snapshot to preserve the state of the system at a point in time. For example, years ago a company that the author worked for required that everything that went into building a software product—operating system, compilers, libraries, source code, build files—had to be archived, along with instructions on how to build the product, before it could be shipped. That way, a future team could rebuild the software if necessary. Creating this package was often a time-consuming process to develop and test. Using virtualization, you simply take a snapshot of the build machine and archive it.

■ *Versioning and Differencing Scenarios.* Virtual machine images allow you to easily update your entire software stack, including the virtual machine, operating system, and applications. As virtual machines proliferate, users will want to know how any two particular virtual machines differ. Just as there are software tools to difference source code files, it should be eventually possible to difference virtual machines.

■ *Staging Scenarios.* Virtual machines can be prepared in advance, ready for use. This could be useful in development and testing scenarios, load balancing in data centers, and so on. In fact, entire catalogs of virtual machines can be created with different software builds.

Disposability

The ability to delete a virtual machine appears in many scenarios such as the following:

■ *Taint and Reset Scenarios.* These scenarios involve the ability to start with a virtual machine image, use it, and then reset it back to its original state. For example, as the Security section described, partitions dedicated to Web browsing can be periodically reset to a known good image to get rid of any accumulated malware. Also, software testing scenarios often require starting from a specific state. Once testing has occurred, it can be repeated by resetting to the original state.

■ *Limited Lifetime and Time-Out Scenarios.* Developers are often reluctant to install new software on their development machines; they don't want to taint a production system with something that might disturb it. A company that wants to encourage developers to try its products can easily prepare an evaluation virtual machine with its software pre-installed.[1] Also, installing an operating system can be a time consuming task. Developers and users are more likely to try an operating system if they don't have to take the time to install it, but can just run a virtual machine image. In fact, they can run multiple versions, side by side, to evaluate them together.

■ *User Education Scenarios.* User education is fertile ground for the use of virtualization. Building on the previous idea, an organization might assemble a packaged image that includes the operating system, tools, and educational materials in a single virtual machine bundle. The image requires no installation and configuration; the student runs the virtual machine and can get started immediately on exercises in a carefully prepared environment.

---

[1] Of course, this is subject to licensing restrictions for the operation system. An open source operating system would make things a bit easier.

▪ *Hands-on Experience/Evaluation Scenarios.* Often people would like to try evaluate software, but don't want to taint their personal machines with software they aren't sure will be free of side-effects. Virtualization allows people to experiment with software without the associated risks.

▪ *"Risky Development" Scenarios.* Some development activities, such as creating device drivers, are best done on "sacrificial" machines. A virtual machine running on a high-powered development platform is a good compromise, allowing the developer to edit and build on the host machine while running the software that has a high likelihood of crashing the operating system in a virtual machine. Risky development activities can be taken on without additional hardware costs.

Conclusion

Virtualization impacts existing usage models for potentially everyone in an organization—including developers, testers, the IT personnel, marketing and sales—and will enable new usages that were not previously possible. To begin to understand the implications of virtualization, this chapter explored the impact of virtualization on common requirements such as security, availability, and reliability. While this approach helps to put virtualization in context, the next section provided more detail by looking directly at the qualities of virtualization, including hostability, platform independence, portability, isolation, duplicability, persistence, and disposability, and listing categories of usage models that they enable.

The next chapter begins the survey of virtualization use cases. In the specific use cases that follow, you will likely identify the qualities of virtualization that they rely on and will hopefully discover new ways to look at the technical problems you face and generate even more applications of virtualization technology.

Chapter 4

Software Development: Developers

I'm consistent. I'm always for my team.

—Grover Norquist

Hardware and software acquisition is not a minor cost for the budding or even the established software development shop. The costs for software and hardware can easily exceed USD 5,000 or sometimes USD 10,000 per developer, when you consider the cost for software licenses on top of hardware.

To take a look at a simple example, let's say that you are a Microsoft-focused development shop in that most or perhaps all of your development utilizes Microsoft tools and technologies. Even with an attempt to make use of a single vendor for all of your development efforts, the costs can be daunting. Each developer will typically need a desktop machine at a minimum, with a decent size monitor. This alone might cost the company USD 2,000 per developer. You might also need a secondary physical machine or laptop to allow a developer to access productivity applications such as email easily, even when the development machine is otherwise occupied or in an indeterminate state due to a current development effort. On top of that, software licenses are cumulative based on the amount of hardware you have. Typically, you might be spending another USD 2,000 or in some cases USD 5,000 *per year* to equip a developer with a full package of software from Microsoft for development and testing purposes, in addition to the software required for machines set up just for productivity and daily use.

Virtualization makes it possible to limit these hardware expenditures. The first way that it does so is by limiting the amount of hardware you have to buy. Depending on the type of license agreement you have for the development software you use, virtualization may allow you to take legitimate advantage of the ability to use multiple licenses for testing and development purposes on the same machine, without occurring additional costs. Note, however, that these types of policies change often, and you should check regularly to ensure what your rights are in terms of development and test licenses.

The rest of this chapter covers some of the key benefits of virtualization as it relates to software development. It also covers the benefits of virtualization from the perspective of managing teams of software developers to achieve a given software development goal. This chapter touches occasionally on testing, which will be dealt with in more detail in Chapter 5.

Managing the Development Process

Any assertion that managing a software development process is easy can be countered by the number of books on the process with titles like *The Software Project Survival Guide.* Managing software projects is not a task for the squeamish, and the stakes can be high.

That said, anything that makes it easier to manage the software development process and ensures greater developer productivity can only be a good thing. This section of the chapter takes the time to explain the benefits that virtualization provides in this area.

Deploying Software Configurations

One common concern with building software applications is ensuring that all of the developers are working with and testing their code against the same base platform. If developers are not utilizing the same builds of tools and associated development applications like source-code control systems during the development process, it is easy for discrepancies to occur. It is also easy for discrepancies to occur if the developers are not using the exact same base operating system, with the same set of service packs and fixes.

Virtualization makes it easy to deploy a single software configuration to all of your developers. For example, you could easily configure a development environment that has the specific service packs and hotfixes you need as part of your mandated base software development platform. Using virtual machines also makes it easy to mandate changes to development tools when new versions of those tools become available.

Whether you are using server-based virtualization or desktop virtualization tools, you can, in nearly all cases, deliver a pre-built virtual machine to a developer faster than they could install the tool updates themselves.

Avoid Installation Hassles

One additional benefit of standardizing on a single base platform image is that installation hassles are removed, avoiding the lost productivity that you would otherwise incur as a result. This benefit means that, instead of distributing a new bug-tracking client, source-code control client, or bug-fixed version of a development environment to all developers as a raw software install, you can now configure once and deploy.

The Issues

Virtualization gives you the opportunity to designate a core group of individuals in your development or IT group to pre-configure development environments for the rest of the software development team and deploy those development environments for immediate use.

In many cases, when deploying the raw software, it may take days or weeks for the entire development team to come up to speed with the new software and to have it installed on their machines. This is especially true if development tools undergo a significant change such as moving from one major development environment version to another, such as Visual Studio[†] .NET 2003 to Visual Studio 2005. In many cases, the updates themselves will take some time to propagate throughout the organization, due to bandwidth considerations or the need to ship physical media. Unfortunately, even after this lag, you will still have to undergo the pain of the physical installation of the new software across a team of developers.

One of the reasons for this pain is that individual developers may vary greatly in their competence and experience installing a given software package. It is not uncommon to have a developer who is exceptional at writing C#, Java, or C++ code but who is beset with concerns and issues when attempting to install a software package. IT skills around installation and configuration of software and those of mainline software development are not always found in the same individual.

An additional concern that needs to be addressed is that individual developers may cause issues by installing personal software on their machines. For example, one developer may have Winamp[†], and another may have MusicMatch[†] or Yahoo![†] Music[†] for listening to music. One developer may have a variety of plug-ins added to their development environment that another developer may not. Any additional software installed on the development machine has the potential to create lost productivity through installation and configuration conflicts. With the deployment of a preconfigured virtual machine with the appropriate development environment and associated mandated applications pre-installed, the installation of personal productivity software is something that can be handled *after* the developer is productive and up and running with the new environment.

This discussion also must take into account valid experimentation by the developers themselves when troubleshooting previous bugs. For example, the developer may have downloaded various hotfixes, service packs, SDKs, and utilities, or they may have configured their base operating system differently than standardized corporate defaults, in an attempt to trace down a previous bug. In many cases, these changes may not have installed side-by-side with previous releases, as it is common, for example, for an SDK that is newer to replace the installation of the older version. All of these changes to the base development platform may contribute to delays in loading the mission-critical software that you need installed, preferably overnight or in a single day, in order to move the development team forward and hit the target release date. Any lag potentially delays the product release cycle, or at least creates areas of low productivity that the rest of the team has to work around.

The Installation and Configuration Team

As mentioned above, virtualization makes it possible to localize the pain of installation and configuration to a designated team. Over time, this team becomes expert at installing various packages that you use or intend to use, and they become proficient at troubleshooting installation issues rapidly. Building this type of specialized knowledge within the organization is valuable, as the installation team can roll out subsequent base configuration changes more rapidly. They can also let the development team stay focused on writing code, instead of dealing with potential troubleshooting around installation or application compatibility issues on the deployed virtual machines.

When leveraging a select group of application installers and configuration setters, you can make better use of internal resources and save time and money.

Personal Productivity Software

In addition to providing the standard development environment to the development team, it is also valuable to provide a locked-down virtual machine already preloaded with all of the necessary productivity software the company uses. This image could be preconfigured with appropriate settings to access corporate mail, web portals, instant-messaging servers, and other network services. In this way, regardless of anything that happens to the developer machine's software state, they are not be limited from using and connecting in discussions through email, IM, and other means. An important consideration here is to lock down this productivity image more thoroughly than a development image, so that developers do not modify it unnecessarily. By limiting this lockdown to a virtual machine and not the host machine or all virtual machines, it is more likely that the developer and other potential users will not try to circumvent the security enhancements to that image, allowing it to be more stable in the long run.

The Role of IT

One of the additional considerations is that developers also need access to internal resources only found on the corporate network. The benefit that virtualization can provide in this area is more completely addressed in other chapters. In the present context, it is worth considering that developers could also be provided with a dedicated machine that is only used for remote access scenarios to the corporate network. This machine could be hardened and only set up to allow actions that would be appropriate when connected outside the corporate network.

Managing Geographically Diverse Teams

In many ways, the UPS or FedEx delivery person can be a significant asset when using virtual machines as part of your development effort. The ability to quickly and relatively inexpensively ship a fully configured machine to a geographically distant development team is a significant boon for both development and testing groups.

One of the issues that can easily arise in developing software applications with diverse teams is that remote development teams can be out of synch with the base development platform. While this circumstance obviously can be resolved through more traditional means, it is much more efficient to "install once and ship anywhere." Using this approach means that widely diverse teams can quickly be up and running with the same development platform, without concerns about individual configuration issues.

This technique also makes it easier for development teams that are geographically separated to quickly get in synch on a similar set of images if, for example, a remote team is developing the middle tier for an application and the local development team is developing the client and server tiers.

This capability brings peace of mind and security knowing that your development team can be easily transitioned to new and more productive tools or versions of tools you currently use, regardless of the organizational structure and location of the development team, without significant lag or loss of productivity in using this model.

This type of usage is not without costs, however. As mentioned in the introductory chapter of this book, one of the limitations of virtual machine technology is that it currently takes a good deal of time to compress, transfer over the network, or burn images to DVD. Moreover, you also have to consider the additional time and expense it might take to get these DVDs ready for shipment, as well as actual shipping expenses.

Another useful distribution technique is to utilize a server-based solution that developers log into remotely. Using a product such as Xen 3.0, GSX, ESX, Virtual Server, or others you can quickly set up a remote environment that developers can log into with a web browser.

Localization

Applications that need to be developed for various audiences around the world are another place where virtualization technologies can play a key role in saving development time. Developing applications for use outside of the locale where they were originally developed can result in a large amount of testing and development work to ensure that the software will work and display appropriately in another geography. For example, the differences in displaying an English-language character set, as opposed to displaying an Asian-language character set, may cause various elements of the screen display to no longer fit appropriately in terms of text on dialogues, labels on the user interface, and messages displayed to the user. To understand the problem in a bit more detail, consider some of the concerns that crop up when developing an application for the global market.

First is the issue of bi-directional awareness, which refers to the need to handle languages that are not read from left to right but are read from right to left. Line and word breaks are another concern, as European languages typically break text on white space such as end of line, punctuation, or tabs. Many Asian languages, for example, do not separate words in this same way, and some, such as Thai, do not use punctuation.

Another issue is the use of shortcut keys in the application, as an arrangement of keys that would make a good shortcut for one language may not be the same for another language. This list of issues associated with deploying an application globally is just a small start. Being able to easily create a bank of virtual machines that can be copied locally or accessed through a server-based virtualization product makes it much easier for a company to add support for languages other than the language for which the application was originally developed. Using virtualization makes it possible in this model to have each machine already preconfigured for a particular locale at a fraction of the cost it would take if physical machines were used to support a large number of different locales. The cost to add additional languages as time passes is also less as the market for the application grows due to the ease at which you can build out a new library of virtual machines and then distribute them out to the development team.

With the market for software becoming ever-more competitive and with the growth of emerging markets, the need for localized versions of software may be expected to increase. Virtualization technologies can help you to easily localize your application for the global marketplace by giving you more flexibility in the deployment and storage of a repository of virtual machines already configured for various locales and geographies.

Software-Development Continuity

One of the largest concerns of software-development organizations both large and small is the safety of the intellectual property that they are developing. This concern pertains not only to theft, but also disaster recovery and business continuity issues. While the IT section of this book covers business continuity scenarios in much deeper detail, it is important to understand here the impact that virtualization can have in software-development shops with regard to business continuity. Especially for smaller shops, virtualization can provide a very quick way of maintaining software development efforts in the event of a significant event that limits access to mainline systems.

Business Continuity

It is critical that development firms can continue to operate in the event of a fire or other emergency that causes loss of property. While it is common for companies to have some type of offsite storage or replication plan in place for critical data, limited work and effort is spent on ensuring that developer and test machines are backed up. The various custom configurations, software installations, and other operating system tweaks are numerous on a given developer's or tester's machine, and re-creating those attributes in the event of an emergency can be prohibitive.

Virtualization technologies can make it easy to produce complete backups nightly of each development and test environment, by backing up the entire set of virtual machines. In this way, if a significant business-interruption event were to occur, such as a fire or natural disaster, the development team would be able to begin development as soon as they were able to copy their virtualized environments from remote storage. Contrast this with having to restore all of the development environments from scratch using a system level backup that would require the same hardware that the backup was taken from in order to restore the backup appropriately. In the case of virtualization all that is needed is generic laptop running an operating system and an installation of virtualization software alone. At that point the portability of virtual machines comes into play. The portability of virtual machines allows you to simply copy the virtual machine to the developer's generically configured laptop and they can begin working again immediately. This also means that, in many cases, the development team may be able to continue working for a period of time with secondary machines or mobile platforms while new office space is acquired, new machines are purchased, and other infrastructure is replaced. The interim machines would simply need to run virtual machines from the last nightly backup that contains all of the work they were working on prior to the precipitating event. In this way, the software-development organization can mitigate the costs associated with idle, nonproductive time and lost-opportunity costs while physical facilities are returned to their normal state.

Contract Development

The use of contract developers or a pool of developers adds further concerns for a software-development organization. These developers need to be supplied with hardware and associated software configurations that match the rest of the development team, even though they may have not been part of the team from the start. With virtualization technology, you can easily supply contract developers with the exact same base configuration as the rest of the team. In addition, contract developers can be supplied with images that have a lower level of built-in permissions than full-time employees have, in terms of access to the corporate network and other policy settings that can be set. Being able to lock down these machines offers more peace of mind when working with contract developers, as well as giving you a very efficient means of providing a properly configured workstation for them to get to work on promptly.

Off-Site Development Work

Many developers value the opportunity to work from home and/or work from diverse locations such as a coffee shop for a morning and increasingly organizations are allowing this type of work environment to proliferate. Additionally many workers increasingly expect this privilege, or at least, it is seen as a significant benefit that the company can provide at limited cost assuming productivity is kept at expected and maintainable levels. Providing this benefit also typically leads to increased employee loyalty compared to companies who do not and assists in recruitment and retention.

While the value of enabling developers to work off-site may be clear, many companies do not adequately consider the hidden costs of a remote work scenario that can be at least partially alleviated through the use of virtualization technologies. The first of these is that most corporations do not track or pay attention to the amount of time lost by developers and other members of the team when they are working remotely. Moreover, these individuals may not have all of the software they need installed or properly configured locally on their host machine. Some of this limitation, of course, is due to the inability for certain software configurations to exist simultaneously on a given host machine.

The cost of a developer working in a remote scenario without being productive can be high, as each hour lost affects the overall development effort. Worse yet, these low productivity issues are typically hidden, because the developer is working offsite, and it may not be clear that they are working at less than 100-percent efficiency in terms of access to all of the tools that they need. One of the benefits of virtualization is that a developer can rapidly configure a mobile computer such as a notebook or Tablet PC to be able to run with a fully configured development environment that contains local copies of the source code, development tools, documentation, and whatever else is necessary to begin coding within perhaps 20 to 30 minutes.

This capability can be supported simply by copying an image they are working on from their desktop machine to their mobile machine before leaving the office. Much more importantly, they can configure numerous environments simply by copying additional virtual machines to their mobile platform. The only thing that is necessary is to copy the image from a desktop machine over to a mobile PC. Considering that most fully loaded development images range from 2 GB to 8 GB, this process can take anywhere from 15 minutes to 30 minutes, depending on the type of network connection available to make the transfer.

This time lag is a small price to pay for ensuring that when a developer goes out on the road to a conference or is simply working out of the office at the local coffee shop, they are working with the same base image as the rest of the team. This consistency across the development effort ensures maximum use of the developer's time, and it helps to continue to provide flexible working locations and hours for the development team, which is increasingly valued by employees.

Cross-Platform Development

Cross-platform development efforts can also be made much easier with virtualization. One of the reasons for this advantage is that being able to do cross-platform development without the benefit of virtualization almost always requires two physical machines.

As a simple example, consider a small ISV that wants to develop a product that will run on both Windows and Linux. The option of dual booting is possible, but that would require the developer to repeatedly and often go through the three- to four-minute process of shutting down one operating system and launching another. Moreover, one must also consider the additional time in each iteration of this process to shut down open applications such as links to development systems and productivity applications before switching to the other operating system. The developer in the non-virtualized scenario also needs to update any local code repositories from remote ones. With this in mind, the process may take on the order of five to seven minutes each time, or perhaps longer. If this process is repeated a few times during the day, the developer can easily lose substantial productivity, in addition to lost concentration when writing code. The developer also needs to ensure that any locally stored data is available to both operating systems, which may mean putting it on a separately formatted drive and maintaining it there.

With virtualization, it is possible to keep a single machine up and running a given host operating system and then to launch numerous different virtual machines running Linux and Windows, respectively. This means that a developer can easily just switch between open windows on a single machine to switch between development environments. Over the course of a large project, the time saved by avoiding loss of concentration, as well as the need to switch manually between platforms can be substantial.

Developers can also easily share resources between virtual machines using functionality that most vendors provide, as discussed in Chapter 2.

Of course, multiple physical machines could be provided, but that solution would make less efficient use of resources, even though it is a source of pride for many people to have a large number of machines in their work area. For the cost of a USD 100 or USD 200 software acquisition and potentially some additional drive space, you can make better use of current hardware by running multiple platforms on the same hardware and still give developers the flexibility of running as many different operating systems and environments as they wish to remain productive.

Encapsulating Production Machines

One of the more interesting uses of virtualization in a software-development environment is the ability to mimic production systems in their totality. This can be accomplished in one of two ways. The first of these would be manual replication where you simply create a replica of the production systems on virtual machines through a manual installation process. The second of these would be to utilize physical to virtual imaging techniques in order to make a set of virtual machines that mimic the production machines. In this way complete and full replicas of the production machines themselves can be easily shared amongst the development team.

Manual Replication

The ability of virtual machines to replicate an entire network topology on a single machine makes it very easy to emulate complex production systems. This capability can be invaluable for software development projects that extend the work effort already put forth to develop complex systems. That value stems from being able to ensure that extensions to existing systems will function correctly upon deployment, which is a significant consideration. Being able to replicate an entire environment on a single developer's workstation or to a separate single server installation makes it much less likely that new software will fail to integrate with existing systems. An additional benefit is that, until the actual moment of production integration, little or no direct interaction is needed with production systems that may be running under service-level agreements that require a dedicated amount of up time.

Using virtualization technologies in this way makes it easy to develop software that you are sure will work right the first time, while letting you keep production machines utilized and running safely for their primary tasks.

Imaging and Virtualization

In addition to a manual installation approach where you simply mimic the production machines in every particular, some virtualization vendors provide an approach that allows you to directly image a production machine and turn it into a virtual machine. This can be a good type of functionality to use when you are unsure whether all of the configuration changes made to production machines over time, including the installation of hotfixes and changes to application configuration files and databases, have been properly documented and saved. With a technology like the Physical to Virtual (P2V) technology that is offered by VMware through their P2V Assistant and by Microsoft through their Virtual Server Migration Toolkit (VSMT), as well as other similar tools, you can quickly and easily image a running production machine and then take that replica image and use it as part of testing and development efforts.

This is an incredibly powerful addition to the toolkit of a company developing custom software solutions. For example, using this method ensures that *all* configuration settings are copied over to the virtual machine.

Working with Legacy Production Systems

The need often exists to develop an enhancement for software that is a few releases old or to develop for compatibility with legacy software, for the benefit of customers that have not upgraded their environments to newer versions of the software. Virtualization gives you the ability as a software development company to quickly produce a virtual machine running the legacy software, even on operating systems and platforms that are no longer directly supported by the manufacturer.

For example you can easily create a series of Windows 95, Windows 98, NT 4.0, or earlier or later Microsoft or Open Source operating system images and install legacy software on them as well such as older versions of productivity and development tools for furthering the development effort or patching older releases.

This ability enables you to save on hardware costs in this use case and also have a much more rapid release cycle for the fix, due to the ability to generate an image much faster than attempting to acquire older compatible hardware.

Professional Services and Custom Application Development

Companies engaged in developing custom applications based on specifications from external customers can gain unique benefits when it comes to virtualization technology. This section outlines some of those benefits in terms of real-time reactions to customer needs, providing support, and being able to respond more quickly to market trends in terms of desired skills.

Customer Support

Typically, when building custom software based on a client specification, a certain number of support hours are made part of the project scope, in order to support the deployment and initial maintenance of the solution. In a fair number of cases, these relationships become ongoing over time, and the professional services firm needs to be able to respond to a variety of concerns that might span months or years between the times contact is made.

Virtualization makes it easier to provide support to current customers who have an ongoing support agreement in situations such as this. For example, you could easily maintain a repository of images that match each customer's configuration to which you have deployed. While this would not be feasible if it were necessary to keep physical machines available with each configuration, it is not all that costly to maintain, especially when you consider that you do not need to have all of these images launched at a single point of time. Therefore, storage resources are the key consideration, rather than overall CPU or memory resources in this case. For example, on a mirrored 250 GB SATA drive (which would cost approximately USD 300 for both drives as of the first quarter of 2006) you could store the following:

■ 55 Windows XP client images with approximately 1.5 gigabytes of application software installed on top of the base operating system.

■ 42 Windows Server 2003 server images with approximately 1.5 gigabytes of application software installed on top of the base operating system.

The above examples assume a base operating system configuration with a standard amount of additional options installed and a relatively large amount of space (1.5 GB) reserved for applications. While a company may never have considered keeping copies of client's production systems based on the time of initial deployment, this type of scenario can be very cost effective with the model shown above. For example the cost per customer configuration is only USD 7.14 for the cost to store each customer's server configuration. Licensing issues obviously have to be taken into account but with many vendors moving to a model where you only pay for licenses that are active at one time this model still does not cost a significant amount of money to maintain if you assume you will have a small amount of the repository of images active at one time in order to address customer concerns.

Considering it costs only USD 7.14 to have a image that matches the original customer configuration stored compared to the typical costs in attempting to set up a system to match that deployed configuration after the fact, obtaining a snapshot of a deployed system using a tool like P2V Assistant prior to moving into a support-contract role with a customer can save an inordinate amount of time in being able to respond to a customer request, compared to the cost involved.

It should obviously be mentioned that a customer's production system will deviate over time from the image that was taken at the start of the project. But even if the configuration changes over time it is much easier to start from a pre-stored series of base virtual machines that already have all of the base software installed and configured as at the time of deployment and make small changes to these virtual machines to bring them in alignment with the current customer configuration. And as will be shown later simply having the original base virtual machines around can have a benefit in and of itself regardless of whether they match the current customer configuration.

On-Site Support

Another consideration associated with using virtualization in the context of providing professional services is the provision of on-site support. If the support contract you have with the customer includes on-site support, you should consider how beneficial it would be to have a copy of the customer's production systems and other working systems resident on the consultant's laptop prior to having them travel to the client site. This capability would also allow the consultant to remain productive if he or she were unable to access the client machines immediately upon arrival, due to their being in heavy use or other considerations.

Loaner Virtual Machines

An additional usage model that may provide significant benefits is using virtual machines as part of a "loaner" model. Many people are familiar with the concept of car dealerships providing you a loaned car during the time of the repair process on your vehicle. In the case where production data can be easily migrated, it might be possible to easily provide the customer a loaned production system that is fully configured while support issues on the production systems are addressed.

Depending whether the customer is already using virtualization in another portion of their organization and has the appropriate licenses, whether you can amortize the cost of the virtualization software as part of the temporary solution are some of the key concerns in attempting to use this model. But even with those considerations in mind, this model has the capability to get the customer up and running with a configured system while the other system is brought offline for investigative purposes.

Sending It Back to the Shop

Another very valuable use case is the obverse of the loaner model discussed above: the ability to capture a customer configuration in a virtual machine and bring it back to your headquarters so that it can be worked on. If you are concerned that the customer configuration may require more of the company's experts than can be reasonably sent to the customer site, this can be the best option. For a professional services firm, it might make it more possible for senior consultants to remain at the home office to help out in other more strategic areas such as client building but still be available to troubleshoot high-priority cases with more junior consultants in a hands-on manner.

Confirming the Source of the Problem

At times when doing custom development, it is difficult to ascertain whether or not the client has made changes to the base deployed configuration, either unintentionally or without documentation. Many times, these changes are at the core of why an application that behaved as expected at installation fails some time later.

If you have made use of a model where you create an image of a customer's production machine prior to leaving the deployment site, you then have the ability to easily perform a differential check between what you have stored away, which is an exact copy of the machines at the time of deployment, and what the customer is running on site. While specific tools don't exist that would let you compare all of the possible changes to a virtual machine side by side, you can very clearly ascertain with the individual products that have installed whether they have been modified in terms of changes to installation paths, registry keys, application configuration files, database settings, and the like.

While the negotiations with the client have to be handled delicately if something is found to be amiss, you at least are in the position of having a better footing when it comes time to have the discussion with your client. The ability to repudiate concerns that the client may have by having a set of images that match the original configuration and were taken onsite at the conclusion of the project can be a powerful tool to have if conversations between the professional services firm and the end client go awry.

Deliver as Virtual Machine

One obvious conclusion that can be drawn out of the above discussion is that you might want to consider delivering custom applications using fully functional virtual machines as the end product. In this way, assuming you can amortize the cost of virtual machine software as part of the package price for the development effort, you might save yourself significant money in support costs, quicker response time, and easier deployment. Those savings may well more than offset the cost of providing the end customer with a license to run an appropriate virtualization product.

Hands-on Experience

One of the additional significant benefits of virtualization from a professional-services perspective is the ability to quickly experiment with new technology. Most professional services firms have to keep consultants up to date about the latest releases of products that they are developing applications for or on. Experimentation with new software releases, however, can be troublesome at best. In many cases, alpha or beta releases of new software from vendors of operating systems, development tools, databases, and so on can be buggy and take significant time to install. They also may fail to work as expected, create instability issues, or cause conflicts with other applications on the machine.

Nevertheless, every professional services firm has to ensure that the consultants they employ are up to date on the latest trends and technologies in order to secure future business opportunities. Moreover, it is not atypical for the consultants themselves to want this type of opportunity, in order to further their own career goals. Lastly, this type of experimentation early in the product cycle makes it easier overall to get around potential implementation barriers of new technology adoption, as those barriers might have been discovered and workarounds found perhaps months prior to an initial engagement with a customer.

Virtualization gives the professional services firm the capability to experiment at will. Consultants can experiment with the latest technologies, whether on the road or in the office, without worry that such experimentation will negatively affect their ability to get billable work done on current projects. Virtualization technologies provide this benefit by their efficient sandboxing of networks from one another as well as the clear separation between virtual machines and between a virtual machine and the host operating system. The knowledge gained can also be more easily shared, as virtual machines preconfigured with the latest releases can be made easily available to all consultants at once.

Application Migration Scenarios

Another useful scenario to consider in terms of the use of virtualization is as a test platform for application-migration issues. In many cases, the migration of a user's active directory from one platform to another (for instance, from Novell to Microsoft), from one email system to another (such as Notes to Exchange), or one database system to another (Microsoft to Oracle, and so on) can be fraught with issues. Many vendors provide migration tools to move from previous releases of their own products to new ones, as well as from competitors' products to help make this process somewhat easier, but providing and testing a migration solution can take significant time.

One way that potential concerns are addressed is to work with representative sample data in test environments. In many cases, however, the migration tools may take hours to run with a data set, and then when errors are found, it may take a number of hours to reset the system to a state where the data is once again ready for a migration test and is ready again to be validated. With virtualization technologies, these types of expensive migration issues can be minimized through the creative use of snapshots, undo files, and multiple virtual machines. The use of these types of techniques makes it possible to easily create an environment that can be quickly rolled back after a failed migration attempt and restarted. This capability potentially saves hours on migration-solution testing prior to an actual attempt on-site at the customer's location.

Development Methodology

It is important to consider the impact that all of the preceding discussion has on development methodology. These days, it is not uncommon for a development shop to practice one form of agile development or another. Whether it is Scrum, XP, or some other derivative, agile development tends to be founded on some basic principles. The following are some excerpts from the AgileManifesto at AgileManifesto.com

- Our highest priority is to satisfy the customer through early and continuous delivery of valuable software.

- Deliver working software frequently from a couple of weeks to a couple of months with a preference to a shorter timescale.

- Working software is the primary measure of progress.

Working with just these excerpts, it can be clearly seen how virtualization technologies can help a company that has embraced agile development efforts.

"...Satisfy the Customer through Early and Continuous Delivery..."

One aspect of the development effort that makes it difficult to deliver software to the end customer is the simple fact that early in the development process, documentation on setup, configuration, and stability issues is generally not available. Regardless of that fact, the customer needs to see the work in progress and have time to explore the software. One possible solution that ensures a stable build and adequate time for the customer to examine the software is to utilize a virtual machine delivery as the core element of the review cycle. This will allow the customer to "take home" the product at a given stage of development and work with it, without having to worry about what is most likely a manual and not completely documented setup and configuration process, simply focusing on the application's functionality.

This approach has the additional benefit of improving the development company's image in the eyes of the end customer, by refining their focus on the functioning product, rather than implementation details such as installation and configuration that will be handled more elegantly later in the development process.

"...Deliver Working Software Frequently from a Couple of Weeks to a Couple of Months..."

An obvious corollary to the above is that virtualization allows you to deliver software more frequently to the end customer and remain focused on the key points at that phase of the application review cycle. In addition the customer can review progress without lengthy install requirements or configuration requirements.

"...Working Software Is the Measure of Progress..."

Virtualization use makes it much easier to have a working "software first" approach to development. As this chapter and others have shown, virtualization makes it easier to create high-quality software more rapidly, which builds quality throughout the various stages of the development process. In addition putting resources toward continuing development efforts as opposed to supporting alpha software is good for everyone involved.

Additional Considerations

What follows are some additional considerations to keep in mind when evaluating the impact that virtualization technologies can have on the development team.

Securing Developer Machines

An important and ever-present consideration with developer machines is how secure they are in terms of their installed software. It is not uncommon for a developer to experiment with a variety of packages from vendors and open source alternatives in an attempt to speed up their development effort. Using a variety of downloaded software packages, however, such as trial versions from various vendors or open-source alternatives, is not without risk to the physical development machines for which the developer is responsible and/or other machines on the network, particularly if a virus or spyware is introduced through these downloaded tools or if the applications themselves create instability.

Through the delivery mechanisms previously discussed, virtualization makes it possible to easily provide developers with images that they can use for experimentation, without using their primary machines for the experimentation effort. This is accomplished in part through the isolation that virtual machines provide as discussed previously.

Improved Time to Market (Up Front)

It is important to consider the benefits that virtualization provides throughout the development cycle and how this can make it much easier to shorten time to market. Software development is always plagued by the challenge of developing the best software possible while not sacrificing the need to ship products at some point in the future. Through the various use cases outlined in this chapter, virtualization can help you to ship product faster while still retaining a high degree of quality. For example imagine a development team that was enabled to do the following:

- Experiment with new techniques and software releases without impinging on development efforts that were underway
- Provided the capability to build out entire suites of production systems all resident on their development machine and/or

accessible through a server-based virtualization model resident on a single endpoint that could be viewed through a web browser.

■ Enabled to communicate more effectively with the end customer through the use of shared environments that are identical in configuration on both ends of the communication

■ Able to avoid nearly all installation hassles and configuration concerns through the use of dedicated install and configuration team

■ Have the freedom to work remotely with additional guarantees of having all of the software appropriately configured for the task at hand

Additional benefits would also accrue through the use of virtualization technologies as has already been discussed but the above list alone would have a significant impact on a development team working more effectively together and more productively toward an end goal.

Working Virtual All the Time

While the discussion so far around software development has focused on the use of virtualization technologies in conjunction with a host machine's installed applications, one might also consider whether going fully virtual is an appropriate decision. In this way, the host operating system is minimized in terms of its direct software installation requirements, and all software is available through preconfigured virtual machines.

While this is clearly a big step, it can make it much easier for enterprises to avoid *any* potential configuration issues with host machines beyond the most basic considerations and make it very easy to copy and replace virtual machines when issues arise, as opposed to going through significant troubleshooting to resolve issues that might arise with full use of a host machine only.

Conclusion

This chapter has covered how virtualization benefits software developers. Developers benefit from virtualization through the portability of images, the ability to easily reset images, the new ways of interacting with customers through virtualization, and the ways that virtualization makes it easier to develop various types of applications. In addition virtualization technologies can lead to a more productive and enjoyable work environment for developers leading to increased enjoyment of the overall development process. For all of these reasons, virtualization can have sustained and lasting impact on the developers within an organization.

Chapter 5

Software Development: Testing

Process is Intelligence getting to know itself.
—Robert Fripp

Testing software is never an easy process or discipline, and building out commercial software for sale presents one of the most difficult testing scenarios. In order to ensure that your software works as paying customers assume it will, a significant effort must be applied to the testing process. Virtualization technologies can offer dramatic advantages with regard to how you handle testing for a software development project and the degree of quality in the final software product.

This chapter opens with some high-level thoughts about how virtualization impacts the testing process in general. Next, it moves to a deeper discussion of virtualization as it can be applied to specific areas in the testing field. Finally, it closes with some additional areas to consider and a discussion of the tools landscape as it applies to software development in general and virtualization specifically.

Testing and Virtualization

Formal process and standardization are the hallmarks of a well executed testing process for a software development project. In addition a consistent and repeatable approach to the testing process is also required. Virtualization makes it easy to enable greater standardization and consistency across the testing effort. It also lowers the number of testing machines you may need and ends up giving a software development company a competitive advantage in being able to test software more efficiently and more reliability with the utilization of virtualization technology.

Ensuring Consistent Testing and Development Scenarios

When interacting with the testing team, it is important to recognize the need to focus on reproducible scenarios, without allowing imprecision with regard to issues such as what software is installed on each test platform, what issues are reproducible in each environment, and so on.

The use of virtualization provides developers the ability to clearly and quickly fix issues and communicate the results, while using precisely the same image that testers are using to debug and track down issues with their code.

This type of clarity vastly simplifies the effort to determine whether a given bug is in the code itself or is caused by some additional environment issue such as additional software being installed on the target machine that was not expected and that is in conflict with the software package being installed. This clarity improves consistency, decreases testing time and cost, and builds in better overall product quality.

Shelving Testing and Development Scenarios

Another common concern is the need to put a development and test scenario on the shelf for access at a later date. This requirement may arise for any of various reasons. For example, the issue may involve a difficult-to-reproduce bug that you want to keep track of, or it may be necessary or desirable to wait for the appropriate technical resource to dig deeper into the issue. You may also have decided to pursue the bug or application error more exhaustively at a later date when you will have some time to research a more in-depth solution.

In any case, the ability to easily save state on virtual machines and store them away for future use is a significant benefit. This benefit is particularly clear when one contrasts this virtual functionality with the difficulties that would be inherent in trying to persist a physical machine or reproduce the scenario in exactly the same manner days, weeks, or perhaps months down the road. In this case, storing a few gigabytes' worth of data on a server is much more cost effective than the time-consuming process of attempting to replicate a bug that might only arise during a complex series of events that would first need to be documented and then painstakingly reproduced each time the scenario is revisited.

Rinse and Repeat

Another positive use of virtualization in terms of testing software is what I call "Rinse and Repeat" virtualization. This is what VMware would call snapshots or Microsoft would call an undo file. Snapshots or undo files give you the ability during testing to quickly revert to a previous state, or in the case of VMware's product, to use various branching series of snapshots for more complex testing scenarios. Being able to persist and then quickly return to a previous state during a debugging session can be invaluable.

For example, you could easily get to Step 7 in a reproduction process for a bug that has 8 steps and then quickly switch back and forth between the end of Step 7 and the actions that make up Step 8 and generate the bug. Virtualization removes the need to re-image a machine using a tool such as Norton Ghost between each test pass or to carry out time-consuming, step-by-step actions to go from Step 1 to Step 7 in this case. In addition, using a Rinse and Repeat process with virtualization ensures that Steps 1 through 7 are completed in the same way each time since the image was saved at the end of Step 7 and previous steps are not prone to manual error upon reproduction later.

Another consideration to keep in mind, as discussed previously in Chapter 2, is that switching between snapshots or undo files takes less than a minute. The time saved is enormous, compared to performing the same series of steps over and over again in an attempt to determine the source of the bug.

Specific Application Benefits

This section addresses some typical application-testing scenarios, as well as some more specialized ones, in order to illustrate how virtualization can be used in various use cases for testing software. The first of these use cases is web-based applications, the second is instant-messaging applications, the third is peer-to-peer applications, and the fourth is mobilized applications.

Testing Web Applications

Testing for browser compatibility requires a wide range of machines running various operating systems, browsers, and so on. Complicating matters further, in many cases multiple browser versions do not run side-by-side on the same platform. For example, Internet Explorer is typically an install-and-replace model with regard to retaining previous versions of the browser on your machine. Therefore, without the benefit of virtualization, you would need three physical machines to run Internet Explorer 5.0, 6.0, and 7.0 under a single operating system. Additional issues arise when you need to test against a variety of browsers and browsers from different platforms. For example, Table 5.1 shows some of the browsers currently in use on the Internet.

Table 5.1 Browsers in Use on the Internet

Browser	User Base
IE 7.0	.05%
IE 6.0	83%
IE 5.0 (Windows and Mac)	2.8%
IE 4.0	.05%
Gecko Based	10%
Opera	.55%

Source: http://www.upsdell.com/BrowserNews/stat.htm (2006)

Table 5.1 doesn't even list other users such as Apple Safari users or users of other Linux-based browsers whose installations you might also need to test against. For example, Figure 5.1 shows VMware Workstation with RedHat Linux running the Mozilla and Opera browsers for Linux side-by-side on a Windows XP Host machine.

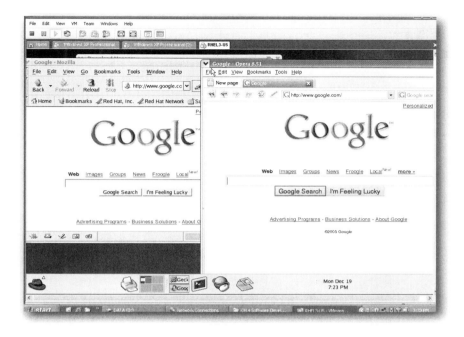

Figure 5.1   Mozilla and Opera Browsers for Linux Running Side-by-Side under VMware

Comprehensive testing is not always feasible when it comes to these scenarios, as the scope of the hardware and software required without virtualization would be tremendous. For this reason, many web applications typically specify a certain set of browsers that they support. Having to test against various browser types and versions, however, and how they render a given Web site, is also in direct opposition to why many software-development organizations might choose web-based development in the first place. For most organizations, the choice to develop web-based applications over desktop ones is made largely because of the perception that application development should be quicker and deployment should be faster than an equivalent desktop project. Moving forward, this concern is becoming more important, as browsers proliferate on small form-factor devices such as cell phones. This trend will increase the test matrix even more.

Software-development companies will become more and more concerned with testing how their web-based applications render on as many different devices and browsers as possible, to increase compatibility. At the same time, however, these same software-development firms must ensure that costs do not escalate out of control when it comes to the testing component of software development for the Web.

Virtualization technologies make it possible to keep entire version histories of browser applications available to be accessed at a moment's notice. Moreover, these images of browsers at various stages of development—such as FireFox 1.0, FireFox 1.5, Internet Explorer 5.5, and Internet Explorer 6.0—make it easy to develop applications that target these browsers and ensure that your Web site will look the same to each user regardless of the browser that they use. While sites such as browsercam.com do exist that let you submit URLs and then receive various renderings of the site in individual browsers, this capability does not change the need to navigate the site independently in the browser as part of the testing and development process. This additional step helps to ensure that Java applets, scripts, cascading style sheets, HTML, and other technologies such as AJAX are functionally correct across all the browsers that might be used to access your site.

Having a bank of virtual test machines at the disposal of the software-testing organization makes it more likely that users will have a positive experience with your site when they access it with the device and browser of their choice.

Instant Messaging

Another consideration for using virtualization software is that it provides a custom application-development organization with the ability to build applications on top of a peer-to-peer model much more quickly. To understand this scenario, consider what a standard application-development environment might look like that is built on top of an instant-messaging framework. For example, assume a scenario where you are building custom bots, or other extensions to an instant-messaging network built on top of Live Communication Server 2005 and Windows Messenger clients.

Bots in this scenario are extensions you can plug into Live Communication Server 2005 that in this case mimic the responses of a customer agent. This kind of solution is sometimes used when you want to route a large number of potential customer-support instant messages to an initial responder that is really not a live agent at all but a background server process that mimics a live agent. In this way, an initial reply is always given while the system sets off on a background thread attempting to find the first available customer service agent and/or simply assigns you to the queue of the next available agent in round-robin fashion after providing a greeting. If you attempt to develop this solution, you are immediately presented with some concerns in attempting to develop the entire solution on a single machine.

Figure 5.2 shows a Windows Server 2003 computer that is running configured as an Active Directory domain controller with the Live Communication Server 2005 product installed. The three client machines are running Windows XP with SP2 and have the latest version of the Windows Messenger client installed.

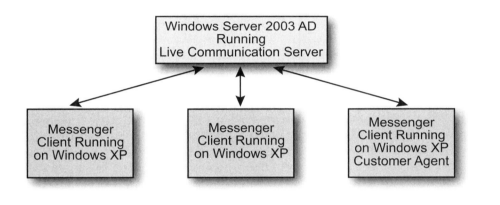

Figure 5.2   A Windows Server 2003 Active Directory Domain Controller and Three Client Machines

This situation is difficult to demonstrate on a single piece of hardware for several reasons. First, the Windows Messenger client cannot have two users logged in simultaneously. While this limitation makes sense from the perspective of the Windows Messenger team at Microsoft, as it would not be a typical scenario to have two different users logged into the same instant-messaging client at the same time on the same hardware, it does present issues when it comes to development. Not being able to log in as two different users simultaneously makes it difficult to determine how the application would respond if numerous requests were received at nearly the same time. Logging in with only one account would make it impossible to test whether or not the Customer Agent was correctly identified when the bot handled the initial instant message. Further, without the ability to log on as multiple instant-messenger accounts at the same time on the same machine, you would be unable to test scenarios where you wanted to confirm that the bot was appropriately distributing new requests across a series of customer agents.

With virtualization technologies, this process is much more straightforward. In this scenario, where processing overhead is minimal for a instant messaging client, you can even have the entire scenario outlined above run on a fairly limited machine and still achieve acceptable performance. This is an advantage compared to the four physical machines in total you would need if you wanted to perform even the limited testing scenario outlined in the diagram. Moreover, you could scale this scenario much more easily with virtualization if you wanted to test 10 or 15 clients accessing the server.

Peer-to-Peer Applications

Peer-to-peer (P2P) applications are another case where virtual machines can provide significant assistance to the development process. To understand this benefit, consider a standard application-development scenario with a P2P product offering. Groove Networks, recently acquired by Microsoft, produced a product that includes P2P file-sharing capabilities, as well as integrated instant messaging. In addition to this client software, they offer a series of server product offerings that integrate with the client product and provide additional administrative tools and greater customizability of network connections between each client. For example, one of their products is a Relay Server that helps control how endpoint information is passed from each client to others that might be available to transfer files. In addition, Groove Networks provides a software development kit that allows developers to extend the application and share data via web service endpoints between client instances of the application.

Developing applications built on a platform such as this could be problematic if each endpoint required physical hardware to test. An application under test can also create conditions that are difficult and costly to recreate when it comes to balancing network traffic issues between the client nodes. Data tends to be transferred in large amounts, and monitoring overall processing overhead for encrypting and packaging the outbound traffic can be very significant. Figure 5.3 shows a typical topology of this type.

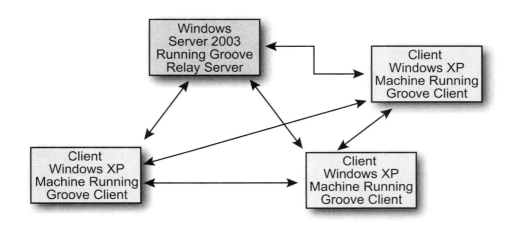

Figure 5.3   A Windows Server 2003 Machine Running Groove Relay Server, with Three Windows XP Client Machines Running the Groove Client

One of the key considerations with P2P technology, as with instant messaging, is that many client applications do not allow multiple user accounts logged in simultaneously on the same client machine. Even if a given application does allow two users to log in simultaneously, doing so might not be a true test of the network bandwidth considerations involved or resources required to perform file transfers, as it may be more typical once deployed to have one user logged on at each node. Testing multiple simultaneously logged-in accounts on the same machine would not be a true test of the load a given machine configuration could handle in terms of CPU utilization for encrypting outbound and decrypting inbound traffic, nor would it accurately represent the network constraints associated with simply sending and receiving the data.

For example, in the scenario above, assume that you are developing a custom application on top of the Groove application architecture, and you are evaluating whether the thousands of dollars required to purchase a Groove Relay Server will truly enhance the performance of the solution. Also assume more on the order of 20 to 25 clients, which is a typically small group of users for Groove. In this case, you can only truly know the impact of the relay server on your solution if you test with numerous client nodes active that are running your custom application and see if the Relay Server provides a significant boost to P2P traffic and local client performance. It is also worth noting that this is the only real way that you can determine whether or not your own application behaves well with that amount of network-traffic load.

Performing such a test with physical machines would cost nearly as much in time, effort, and dollars expended to acquire and set up physical machines for multiple clients as it might take to purchase the additional product in this scenario. Even if it is simply a test of your own application, the costs to truly test a scale-out scenario are enormous, if physical hardware needs to be utilized.

Virtualization allows you to determine easily how your application is behaving in this scenario, even when you scale up to 20 active nodes or more, because all that is required is an additional copy of a virtual machine to be created on disk.

Network Bandwidth and Mobilized Applications

An interesting additional consideration, when developing and testing mobilized applications, is the need to test what will happen when bandwidth is limited in some specified manner. It is often considered appropriate to assume a dedicated level of connectivity for an application that is deployed internally. It is more problematic to make such assumptions for one that connects to the corporate network from an external source. All bets are typically off in terms of the persistence of the connection, its overall bandwidth capabilities, and how much these quantities might fluctuate over a period of time.

Virtual Networks

Many applications today that have been out for at least three to five years have limited ability to deal gracefully with changes to network bandwidth that are drastic or frequent. Even many more-recent applications are not much better in terms of responding to changes in network connectivity. While tools such as the Intel Mobile Platform Software Development Kit are available to help mitigate and respond to network connectivity loss or degradation, many software-development companies do not take advantage of these tools, for a variety of reasons. One of these reasons is an inability to efficiently test for network connectivity loss or degradation and do so in such a way that it does not require specialized hardware for each developer and tester or constant manual switching from one network to another.

With virtualization software, you can easily put together a solution where bandwidth is throttled to each virtual machine. As shown in Figure 5.4, many virtualization products allow you to easily set bandwidth limitations in their user interface.

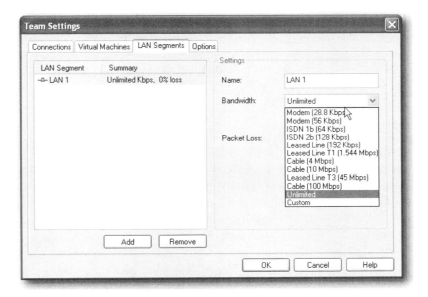

Figure 5.4   Setting Bandwidth Limitations in a Virtual Machine User Interface

The screen capture shown in Figure 5.4 illustrates the creation of a virtual network segment for a VMware Workstation Team. You can easily set a specified amount of virtual bandwidth for the connection, as well as the amount of packet loss.

By creating virtual network segments such as these, it is easy to create network conditions that illustrate the lowering of network bandwidth as an application running in a virtual machine moves from one network segment to another, all while remaining on one physical piece of hardware.

Due to the nature of virtual network interfaces, it is also very easy with many vendor toolsets to create scripts that simulate the loss and reconnection of various network interfaces over a period of time. Being able to do so is obviously preferable to some type of hardware solution that creates a similar end result but requires the purchase of dedicated hardware.

Shaping Network Bandwidth

It is also possible, by using certain server virtualization products, not just to determine whether a network connection is available and to set the fixed bandwidth available to that connection, but to also shape the network bandwidth available to the virtual machine. For example, you are able to set parameters such as the average bandwidth available, the peak bandwidth, and the burst size. The amount of network bandwidth to an application typically varies a great deal beyond simple parameters such as whether or not the application has a connection and the speed of that connection.

Thus, the ability to configure network settings at this granularity and pin those configurations to multiple running virtual machines can speed up development and testing significantly. Most importantly, being able to perform this type of testing using real-world conditions makes it much more likely that the application will behave appropriately once it is released. For example, many applications give users the option to specify different actions that should occur when bandwidth is limited. Figure 5.5 gives an example of such a dialog box in Microsoft Outlook. Notice the options to specify whether a given network protocol will be chosen, based on available bandwidth.

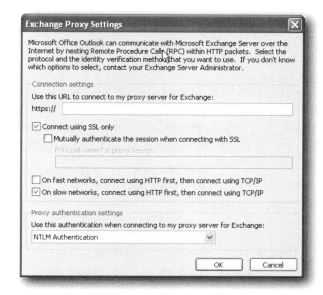

Figure 5.5   Specifying a Bandwidth-dependent Behavior in Microsoft Outlook

Consider a hypothetical case where a company is developing a solution with capabilities such as these, and particular values were encoded as to what the application should do when a fast or slow network was detected. One efficient way to test this behavior would be to test the application on a virtualized set of operating systems and application installs that allow the tester to easily tweak bandwidth settings and shape bandwidth appropriately. This capability would easily let the tester know if the application was appropriately switching back and forth between the HTTP or TCP/IP protocols, and at what points. This information could then be compared with the application specification, and any discrepancies could be pointed out to the developer and then corrected.

Being able to set parameters such as these and easily persist them all as part of a virtualized solution on a single machine makes it easy to diagnose issues during software development or testing of mobilized applications.

Testing for Security Bugs

Virtualization also carries the benefit of being able to easily test conditions that might be dangerous or counterproductive if done on physical machine. For example, if you are a vendor of an anti-virus product or anti-spyware product, using virtualization technologies, you can safely test detection and cleaning routines without resorting to using a physical machine for the testing. In addition, once you are done with testing, you can simply delete the virtual machine with no worries that a product you have in development may not have actually cleaned an infected system successfully.

Scripting and Automation

Many virtualization vendors provide some type of scripting support in their virtualization applications. This section covers how that virtualization support can best be utilized as part of an application-development effort. Some of the following capabilities may be supported by a given vendor, and other functionality may not, but the following should give you a good understanding of the potential use cases for scripting when utilizing virtualization.

Network Monitoring

As mentioned in the previous section, various options exist for configuring network settings, such as disabling and enabling network cards programmatically. These options can be run in sequence in order to simulate particular network conditions. This would allow you to setup a sequence of events where network connectivity is enabled and disabled to simulate a loss of network connectivity event to an application.

Managing Disk Drives

With the various scripting packages, it is easy to add and remove DVD drives from the system, as well as to remove hard-disk connections and other storage connections.

Snapshots and Undo Files

Scripting APIs from various vendors allow you to easily script out a sequence of events using applied snapshots, and then after reporting on the outcome of those events, to undo those events for another test pass. This allows you to easily create a repeatable series of events that are played out across a single virtual machine or multiple virtual machines.

Launch Conditions and Sequences

You can also easily set up specific virtual machines to start first, second, third, and so forth as part of a team of virtual machines that make up an entire solution. You can also pause and restart virtual machines at will, if that is required. This allows you to set up groups of virtual machines that operate in tandem and can be launched in an appropriate order as deemed necessary by product specifications and the test being performed.

Configuring Virtual Machines

With various scripting libraries and web service APIs, you can also perform actions such as creating a virtual machine, deleting a virtual machine, saving state of virtual machines, and similar operations. This allows you to quickly utilize virtual machines for brief test passes and then remove them from disk. Or to simply follow the process of deletion with copying another testing image from a repository of previously unmodified test images.

Automated Testing

Virtualization amounts to a treasure trove of capabilities for the testing group in a software development company. The ability to script and execute the types of operations listed above that previously would have required manual intervention coupled with the previously listed benefits of a virtualization for an organization whose primary responsibility is testing software is very significant. Scripting and SDKs from the various virtualization vendors are an important ingredient in maximizing the value of virtualization. To understand this impact, consider the following scenario. First, a virtual machine is started that is loaded with Windows Server 2003 and is preconfigured as a domain controller, already preloaded with sample users, organizational units, and so forth. Second, a virtual machine is started that is a client of that domain. Assume that the second machine is running Windows XP Professional, which is set to automatically log in to the domain controller for the purposes of the test.

Timing is critical for the test run. The Windows Server 2003 machine must be up and running with all directory services started before the Windows XP machine is launched, or else the Windows XP machine will fail to log in to the domain controller. Setting up this type of sequencing can be easily done using the various SDKs and scripting toolkits provided by the various vendors in the virtualization market. Next, assume that an application has already been preconfigured to connect to the Active Directory domain controller and to retrieve information from the Active Directory for security purposes. This could be an application that is using the LDAP interfaces to query Active Directory about user information.

Even in this simple test, consider the manual steps required without the benefit of scripting support:

1. Start the first virtual machine manually.

2. Wait for visual indication that all services have started and the domain controller has completed its boot up process.

3. Start the second virtual machine manually.

4. Log into the second virtual machine that is a client of the domain.

5. Start the application manually.

If an error were found and you wanted to run the test again, you would need to perform the following steps:

1. Revert to a previously taken undo file or snapshot for the client machine and shut it down.

2. Revert to a previously taken undo file or snapshot for the server machine and shut it down.

3. Repeat the process listed previously to restart the test.

All of these actions, including restart and shutdown, can be completed via the scripting APIs and various SDKs supported by the virtualization vendors. Removing the necessity of having a dedicated person on staff waiting for each machine to log in, wait for a boot sequence, wait for a shutdown or reset sequence, and manually perform all these steps can save a significant amount of money in the overall testing process. This savings is particularly significant if you replicate a scripted or programmatic process across all of the test cases that may be utilized as part of a software testing effort.

While it could be argued that, in this simple example, scripting and SDK support provides only incremental benefit, consider what would happen if the software development company needed to test any or all of the following:

■ What if the software development company needed to test on all of the client operating systems that Windows Active Directory supports, assuming that other operating systems than Windows XP were targeted for the client application?

■ What would happen if the software development company needed to determine whether the application would behave gracefully if the domain controller were not available, such as in the event of the loss of a network connection on the client *or* server? Note that this process could easily be scripted to simulate the loss of network connectivity.

■ What would happen if the software development company needed to persist the state of an error across all machines by cataloging and storing the machines themselves?

■ What if the software development company wanted to test software installation on the client machine and this required a reboot before running the application?

All of the scenarios above would vastly increase the amount of time involved in terms of human intervention and delay the testing and associated development process if the steps were performed manually without virtualization and automation techniques working in tandem. In all of these areas and many others, the pairing of virtualization technology with an in-depth SDK and scripting library can make it very easy to create customized testing solutions that run themselves, save machine state as needed for further review, and then report out results.

Test Labs

While much of the previous discussion has focused on the testing process itself and how virtualization benefits that process, many companies have invested significant amounts of effort into the physical aspects of their test labs. This section addresses some of the benefits virtualization brings to the test lab in particular.

Remote Test Labs

One of the most significant benefits of virtualization when it comes to testing is the ability to create virtual and remote test labs. When your organization grows, or if you simply wish to leverage offshore testing resources (as is becoming more common), building out a virtual lab makes it easy to perform testing on various platforms remotely through a web-browser interface.

A company of sufficient size that is going to leverage virtualization should plan to build out a virtual test lab at some point, as the cost of deploying images to each tester's machine begins to add up and can be easily mitigated by moving to a server-based model for virtualization. In addition, the use of server virtualization makes it possible to store a variety of images and to scale up storage space more effectively on the server side. All of this benefit comes without any loss in productivity for the developers and testers involved in the software-development project.

Local Virtual Labs

Another significant benefit of virtualizing test labs is their portability. Even an average 250 GB USB drive can contain approximately 55 images of Windows XP loaded with 1–1.5 GB of application software. While it would not be possible to launch all of these images at the same time, the ability to have a developer or tester carry with them an entire testing lab in a box is a very powerful benefit of virtualization.

Scalable Test Labs

In addition, by building out a server-based model for testing using virtualization technologies, you can take great advantage of scalable technologies such as multi-core CPUs. Generally speaking, in an era of two, four, eight, and more execution cores being packaged in a single CPU, being able to scale out and take advantage of the processing power available in a single machine is a significant benefit.

Related to this discussion is the fact that most test-lab machines that are not using virtualization technologies are not heavily utilized, and in many cases, they are poorly utilized in terms of hardware consumption. Take the simple example of a test lab required to test five different configurations of Windows XP with various combinations of service packs and hotfixes applied. Let us assume that it is not possible either due to time constraints or the need to test concurrently with all variations up and running on the network to dual-boot, or in this case quintuple-boot, all of the operating systems on the same machine. When this test is running, unless the software is a resource-intensive application, each of the physical machines will experience low utilization of their CPU, memory, and hard disk, as well as other resources such as network utilization. Buying test machines that cost USD 1,000 to USD

2,000 and not utilizing them well is waste that any software development company can do without. Virtualization technologies make it possible to improve utilization.

Electricity, Cooling, and Storage Costs

The costs of a test lab go beyond the basics of purchasing the machines and loading them with the appropriate software. Setting up a test lab also involves ensuring that you have appropriate power and cooling for the machines. In many cases, the costs for power and cooling can be a significant amount compared to the original purchase price of the hardware. In addition, the cost to supply power to a given physical machine increases over the life of the machine. This situation will only continue to increase in significance over time, as computing power and associated electricity and cooling costs increase.

In many cases, a small company could have a fully functioning test lab, perhaps testing more scenarios than previously, and have it all run on one or two servers, achieving a significant savings in electricity costs and physical space. Larger companies potentially could enjoy larger benefits.

Savings on Configuration and Headcount

The simple fact is that software development is an expensive business and is not allied with guarantees of return on investment. The ability to save money and time must always be considered when developing software, and considering that testing and other parts of the organization sometimes get less of the pie in terms of total dollars allocated to the development effort, it is important to stretch those dollars as far as possible. Virtualization makes it possible for all the reasons previously mentioned to save on time, as configuration of a physical machine and setting it up can be reduced to a file-copy operation. Virtualization also helps to save on the headcount that sets up and maintains the test labs for this reason, by virtue of needing fewer machines when virtualization is in use.

Securing the Test Lab

The amount of money invested in the test lab even with virtualization technologies in place is not minor for most companies. Ensuring that these machines are patched on a regular basis and are secure from intrusion is an important consideration. Virtualization makes it possible to increase security through some means that are tailored to virtualization.

Isolation over Protection

One of the considerations of virtualized images is that you can easily restrict the virtual machine from access to certain types of underlying hardware, such as USB devices, floppy drives, and so on. Being able to focus on isolating machines adds value, especially when paired with defense in depth, as described in the next section.

Defense in Depth

Instead of having to secure an entire series of physical machines, you can easily create a series of gold-standard virtual machines that are secure, while frontline machines that contain a copy of the gold standard machines are used for development and testing. In this way, even if your frontline machines are compromised, you have not lost anything except the time required to restore the test lab from the virtual machine store. This process can be easily automated.

Network Isolation

With the methods discussed previously, it is easy to create virtual network segments that allow or deny connectivity outside the host machine for the virtual machines. Most virtualization software also allows you to easily change setting in terms of IP address ranges, whether or not NAT and similar measures are used.

Quicker Lab Quarantine

You can also quickly execute a shutdown of entire systems simply by turning off one bank of virtual machines and bringing another set from storage rapidly. The same can be said for the switching of networks for a running set of virtual machines.

Test Lab Considerations

When it comes to configuring a test lab, some hardware considerations should be kept in mind. The first of these is that, as mentioned in the first chapter, hard-disk utilization is going to be the same whether you choose a virtualized solution or a physical one. That is, the amount of disk space that would have been required to store all of the operating system installs and application installs you had previously remains the same. The key difference is that with a virtualized solution you can scale up a set of machines and not leave storage underutilized on each test machine.

The second hardware consideration in setting up the test lab using virtualization is that you need to be able to utilize CPUs that scale up to the load of multiple operating systems and their associated applications operating concurrently. Multi-core processors can help address this problem by giving you more computing power on a single machine. In addition, some server-based products support the ability to assign a processor to a given virtual machine, thereby giving you the flexibility to assign resources as appropriate to virtual machines.

The third of these hardware considerations is that you need to scale memory appropriately for each test machine, as you will be using memory separately on each virtual machine, with no sharing, as compared to a single physical machine approach. This is one area where 64-bit hardware can be a large help. Being able to apply more than 2 GB of RAM total to applications running on the host, which is the limit for a 32-bit operating system, is vital when running in a virtual environment with numerous virtual machines operating concurrently.

Tools Landscape

Beyond the tools provided by some of the virtualization vendors such as VMware, Microsoft, and XenSource, a variety of third-party tools are worth looking into. This section provides a representative list of some of the different functionality you might find available in third-party virtualization tools.

PlateSpin[+]

PlateSpin (www.platespin.com) provides a variety of products that target the production machine-imaging solution discussed in the chapter focused on Developers. PlateSpin PowerConvert[+] is a powerful, operating-system-level portability solution that lets you easily migrate running virtual machines from one system to another to facilitate various system maintenance or migration scenarios, whether the endpoint is a virtual, physical, or image archive. For example, with PlateSpin, you have no limitations on whether you are moving from a physical to physical server, virtual to physical, or physical to virtual. They also have a variety of other tools that extend the physical, virtual, and image migration story have value in extending the virtualization story for developers and testers.

Akimbi Systems

The Akimbi Slingshot[†] product is a complex configuration capture and restore system that leverages virtualization technology. The product has direct applicability to development and test scenarios. Building on both the Microsoft and VMware products, Akimbi Slingshot provides the capability to persist the complete state of a series of virtual machines that are all part of a given solution and store this state for later retrieval. This gives a development and test team the ability to store an entire collection of related virtual machines in their conjoined state at one time. In this way you could have an entire three tier application with a virtual machine for the client, middle, and data tier all persisted at the same time. In addition all three machines can be retrieved as a unit quickly as well. The product also allows these stored configurations to be easily deployed to server endpoints so they can be accessed by the development team. The tool also allows you to easily start, stop, and pause virtual machines as a unit.

IBM Rational System

One of the more interesting product integrations when it comes to virtualization and developer and tester use cases is the integration of VMware's products with IBM's Rational products. The IBM Rational and VMware Test Lab Automation Solution combine some of the testing benefits of Rational Test Manager with GSX Server from VMware. To understand the integration, a little background is necessary on each product. The Rational Test Manager product from IBM allows you plan for tests, configure them, and automate execution and reporting. Having a tool such as this or one from another vendor, however, doesn't alleviate one of the more time-consuming manual tasks that exist without using virtualization: that of setting up the machines in the test lab for a given test run. By creating a virtual-server–based set of machines, you can then integrate this server-based environment with the capabilities of Rational Test Manager to get an fully end-to-end solution in terms of creating test cases, executing those test cases, launching the appropriate virtual machines to run the test cases, and then reporting back out on the results.

LeoStream

LeoStream (www.leostream.com) provides for both Microsoft and VMware a series of solutions around provisioning virtual servers, including the business processes of virtual server ordering and approval. In addition, LeoStream provides real-time performance monitoring and reporting, policy based access control through extensions to Microsoft's Active Directory, and integrated failover scenarios for virtual servers. The policy-based control allows a development or testing team to set specific limits as to who can power a virtual machine on or off, as well as limits to other operations such as cloning and moving the virtual machine.

Conclusion

In this chapter the discussion has focused on the role of the tester in a software development organization. Various use cases for the virtualization have been presented as they relate to the role of a tester within an organization. Testers can benefit from virtualization technology by build robust applications with less overhead in terms of time, cost, and manpower than before when virtualization is leveraged as part of the testing process.

Chapter 6

Software Development: Marketing, Educating, and Selling

To give yourself the best possible chance of playing to your potential, you must prepare for every eventuality.

—Steve Ballesteros

Developing excellent software involves far more than simply creating a smart development team, appropriate development processes, and a valuable product. It also involves reaching out to potential customers and giving them the reason to buy. Virtualization can help you to better explain your product's capabilities and do so with less risk than if you simply distributed production versions of your software on a trial basis.

Virtualization provides help throughout all aspects of marketing, from educating users to actually selling the product. In this chapter, you will see how a company can take advantage of virtualization technology to help promote their product and get it purchased by more customers than they might have otherwise.

Business Development and Marketing

Virtualization provides the ability to demonstrate the functionality of software while removing the need to configure host systems by abstracting that functionality. This ability enables sales engineers and prospective customers to use the software without having to configure the systems that underlie it, as well as minimizing the necessity of installing the software itself. What's more, virtualization in this context removes the necessity of providing sufficient hardware to demonstrate or evaluate the product, which can be particularly significant for setups that would otherwise require large numbers of systems. Traveling sales professionals and people demonstrating products at conferences benefit tremendously from this.

Another significant advantage of this layer of abstraction is that, since you can create virtual snapshots for various application states, it is possible to step through a demonstration faster than real-time execution would allow, as well as to skip around through the execution path at will. This capability enables demonstrators to tailor the pace and flow of the demonstration according to the needs of the audience.

Virtualized environments are also gaining ground as an option for distributing production software. This model has significant implications for the distribution of sample copies of software, such as take-home copies from a conference, as well as for final sales. The latter option is an emerging model that enables companies to purchase products and to implement them more easily than would otherwise be possible, since that implementation requires little or no configuration.

Tradeshow Demonstrations

One obvious opportunity for using virtualization is in tradeshow demonstrations. Tradeshow costs can be one of the more expensive items in a software development company's budget for marketing expenditures. When you add up the costs of sending two or more employees across the country, shipping computers and other equipment to the show, paying for the booth, and various other expenses, tradeshow expenses can range from a few thousand US dollars for a local event to tens or even hundreds of thousands for remote events at which the company has a high profile.

Virtualization technology can help the company that is developing software take greater advantage of their expenditures associated with tradeshows. Let's take a look at why this is so. The typical tradeshow audience has the following characteristics:

- Limited time to spend per booth.

- Limited patience for long-running demos that don't get to the point.

- The need to understand everything they will take away from the booth within a few minutes.

- Limited patience for demos that fail or exhibit errors.

The software development company exhibiting at the show, on the other hand, typically has objectives such as these:

- A desire to get the attendee to spend as much time as possible watching the demonstration.

- A strong emphasis on getting the customer to see the relevant portions of the software as soon as possible.

- The need to ensure that attendees see the software in the best light possible.

When demonstrating your software product at tradeshows, it is critical that all demonstrations are of the highest quality, get to the point quickly, make efficient use of setup and shipping costs, and *do not fail*. Let's take each of these in turn and see how virtualization can help.

Of the Highest Quality

One of the greatest determinants of a high-quality demonstration is the ability to ensure that the demonstration performs the same way each time. Virtualization provides you the benefit of a virtual machine or a set of virtual machines that have the same look and feel each time they are used. Many times, a demonstration can be crippled simply by the lack of a clean interface or a cluttered demonstration machine that is filled with a variety of nonessential software, such as personalized productivity applications installed by the sales engineer running the demonstration.

Demonstrations can also fail due to a lack of professionalism in terms of the format of the delivery of the demonstration. This issue can be mitigated by allowing the presenter to configure their host machine according to their preferences, with personal choices for screen savers, background wallpaper, installed applications, and so on, while isolating those personal choices from the pre-configured virtual machine. Too many demonstrations have gone awry due to factors such as instant-message popups, email notifications, or screen savers loaded with non-demonstration content appearing in front of potential customers.

Virtual machines can also be easily "branded" with custom themes, custom wallpaper, and screen savers specific to the demonstration and event, and those features can easily be locked down to ensure that they will not be inadvertently switched.

While you could also do the same thing to a non-virtual host machine, the key capability of doing so in a virtual machine is that, by constraining these settings to the virtual machine alone, the presenter is still able to utilize personal settings on their host machine. Meanwhile, a company is able to retain an appropriate corporate theme in terms of screen savers, wallpaper, and other look-and-feel components while the demonstration is executing.

Getting to the Point Quickly

While at first glance it might not be obvious how virtualization makes it simpler to get to the point quickly, it can be a significant help in that regard. The use of "Snapshots" (VMware[†]), "Undo Files" (Microsoft[†]), or similar technology makes it easy to build a demonstration that rapidly moves through a series of preconfigured demonstration steps.

Especially with the use of a feature like the multi-step snapshots in the VMware Workstation product, you can quickly step through a series of application configurations. While doing so might take only a few mouse clicks with virtualization, it would require significantly more effort on a series of host machines. For example, Figure 6.1 illustrates how multiple snapshots allow for easy navigation between various service pack installations and hotfix installations on a Windows[†] XP machine.

Figure 6.1   The VMware Workstation Multi-step Snapshots Feature

Complex IT products such as Systems Management Server or HP OpenView are exceptional candidates for using virtualization in this manner. Many of these products require numerous, complex steps to be executed in order to see the final result, such as a delivered and installed software package on an end-user computer delivered by one of these tools. Additionally, many software packages that are more complex have built in intervals during which the product waits for a specific event before checking for updates or proceeding to the next step in execution. These waiting periods can become extremely awkward to watch in a demonstration context, as the presenter has to fill time waiting for the software to catch up before moving on to the next processing step.

With the aid of virtualization, you could easily build a series of paused virtual machines that are at various stages of the demonstration flow, or even use snapshots to make changes to the application by simply reloading snapshots of the demonstrations at critical stages.

Virtualization technologies in this case make it easy to quickly jump ahead and back to relevant portions of the demonstration that are of key interest to the customer, without bogging down in configuration steps. Consider, for example, the scenario illustrated in Figure 6.2, which depicts a virtualized demonstration environment made up of multiple systems for marketing a monitoring software package. The product being demonstrated monitors remote servers for performance characteristics in terms of CPU, memory utilization, and total connections to a given server from client machines.

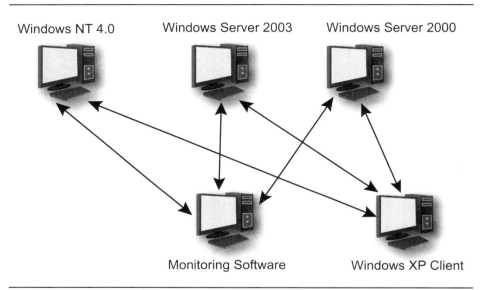

Windows NT 4.0   Windows Server 2003   Windows Server 2000

Monitoring Software   Windows XP Client

Figure 6.2   A Demonstration Environment with Multiple Virtualized Systems

Virtualization allows the creation of an environment for this demonstration with three virtual machines that each run a different operating system—in this case, Windows Server 2003, Windows 2000 Server, and Windows XP. The demonstration could then quickly launch a fourth virtual machine that is running Windows Server 2003 and the management console. Next, you could have your management console connect to all of the other machines that are active.

At that point, you could use snapshots to move each of the machines easily through various states of operation. For example, on the Windows 2000 Server machine, the initial state could be a machine that was not experiencing a high load of CPU activity and memory utilization. You could then roll forward to a snapshot that had multiple applications already executing against that server from the Windows XP client machine. You could then do the same thing for the Windows Server 2003 machine. Finally, you could move the Windows XP machine forward in time, using snapshots to illustrate a scenario where the

Windows XP machine had opened up numerous additional connections to both servers.

You could easily accomplish all of this demonstration using the management console running on the Windows Server 2003 image. In this way, you can quickly progress through the steps of your demonstration, showing just the key points of increased server access and higher utilization from the client machine and focusing on the key points of what your management and monitoring solution can do for the end customer.

Saving on Configuration and Shipping

Shipping costs can be considerable when setting up demonstrations for tradeshows. This cost can be all the more excessive due to restrictions on which vendors you can use for shipping at a given event. Particularly for a large, complex demonstration that involves large amounts of equipment such as several racks of servers, provisioning a booth can be a costly undertaking.

In addition, you incur additional risk each time demonstration machines are delivered. The wrong machine could be allocated, it could be improperly configured, it could be misplaced, or it could fail to be shipped within the appropriate timeframe. Issues such as these keep many a tradeshow coordinator up at night.

By obviating many of the complex hardware requirements associated with such demonstrations, virtualization simplifies these issues tremendously. Virtualization makes it possible to demonstrate an incredibly complex series of relationships between systems with various operating systems and application configurations, using data housed on a single removable hard drive that can be carried easily in a laptop bag.

It is important to note that running these images with the necessary performance may require more hardware than a single computer. Nevertheless, a high-end laptop can usually comfortably run three virtual machines at the same time (and certainly at least two), with more than acceptable performance. In addition, if the demonstration is a simple one-machine configuration, you can easily demonstrate it directly from almost any notebook computer loaded with virtualization software.

The key point to consider here is that virtualization removes the need to ship a series of computers with complex setup and networking requirements. This practice saves a company from the potential risk of only receiving a portion of the demonstration machines, as well as saving on shipping and setup costs. Moreover, setup at the event is far simpler and less prone to error.

Work Without Failure

One of the most significant benefits of virtualization with regard to tradeshow demonstrations is the ability to ensure the success of the demonstration through enhanced testing and shelving.

Using virtualization provides more robust testing scenarios and the knowledge that once tested and shelved, the demonstration will work the same way every time it is run. With virtualization, you can store the virtual machines "on the shelf" using a network drive and pull them off as appropriate for a conference. This type of shelving of the entire platform for demonstrations provides significant peace of mind in the knowledge that the next time you give a demonstration, it will perform identically to the last time.

Another benefit of using virtualization instead of physical machines with preconfigured software is the ease of being able to move virtual machines to another physical machine if the primary demonstration machine starts experiencing hardware problems part way through the tradeshow.

Distribution Models Using Virtual Machines

One of the things to consider with virtualization is that you have the ability to easily distribute, given appropriate licensing considerations, virtual machines to potential customers or current customers interested in upgrading to later releases. This section takes a look at some of the possible models for distribution in this manner.

Take-Home Demonstrations

One important benefit that virtualization provides vendors developing open-source solutions is the ability to set up demonstrations on virtual machines and then provide them on DVDs for customers.

Conventionally, it would be risky and perhaps dangerous to the sales cycle to provide customers this type of direct access to the software early in the relationship-building process. This is especially true in the case of a complex product, where the risk that the user would have a negative experience due to incorrect configuration or installation choices is high. Virtualization technology mitigates these risks, however, due to the ability to deploy the software as a packaged solution already preconfigured and with installation complete.

Distribution of Open-Source Software

Software developed to run on an open-source operating system can be easily distributed using virtualization technology. The ability of open-source software to be freely distributed makes it an excellent candidate for this type of distribution model. It becomes easy for users to have hands-on experience with your software, while mitigating the complexity generally associated with the configuration of open-source software. Releasing both software vendors and potential customers licensing fees for demonstration purposes is a substantial advantage.

Distribution of For-Fee Software

Demonstration software developed to run on a vendor's fee-licensed platform is generally not a viable option for distribution using virtual machines. For any type of freely distributed demonstration content, the costs to provide a virtualized demonstration would be too high per potential user. Most products from Microsoft, Oracle, and other for-fee software vendors fall into this category. Due to the licensing considerations around the Microsoft operating system (as understood at the time of this writing), you would not be allowed to package up demonstrations in this way unless you paid for a license for each person to whom you distributed a demonstration virtual machine.

In cases where software built on top of for-fee architectures is sold at a high enough cost to offset the outlay, virtual machines might be viably distributed in this manner. In such cases, the distribution of demonstration packages could be limited to key decision makers at the later stages of the sales cycle. In some cases, this model might also be viable when the product is ready for customer evaluation, as discussed in a later section.

Disk on Key

One other mechanism that bears mention concerns the fact that, with the ever expanding size and shrinking cost of USB disk-on-key devices, you may be able to utilize this delivery model as well. The rapidly growing sizes and decreasing cost of these devices will increasingly make them a viable medium for distributing virtual machines in the near future.

This development means that, for software that you can distribute using disk-on-key media, you may be able to remove even the file-copy step that is required to distribute a DVD of the software and associated demonstration. In this model, all that is required is that the user has a USB port on their computer and the disk-on-key you provided them to run through a demonstration of your software. When one considers that copying the contents of a virtual machine-based demonstration from DVD to a local disk can easily take 5–10 minutes, and often as much as 20 minutes, this modality has the potential for substantial convenience advantages. The main limitation, of course, is the ability to fit the entire image onto the disk-on-key device.

One final point about take-home software demonstrations is that they enable you to enable potential customers to use a full-function version of your product very easily. While this does come at some cost to ensure that the demonstration is well documented, it can have a much more significant impact than a second-hand demonstration, such as an animated demo on a DVD. The key virtual-machine advantage is that the potential customer is actually using your product and not simply seeing a demo of how it *might* be used. This capability can make a vital difference, particularly in the early stages of the sales cycle.

Virtualization Software

At this point, it is useful to turn to a discussion of the virtualization software itself. While you would be constrained from using certain virtualization software packages due to licensing considerations, some solutions are *not* constrained in this manner, such as the VMware Player discussed earlier in this book and the Xen 3.0 product. Both of these products provide wide freedom in terms of distribution and provide the ability to provide take-home demonstration solutions. To learn more about the VMware player and the Xen 3.0 product, review the material provided in Chapter 2.

Sales Presentations and Demonstrations

A significant concern of every company selling complex software is that, at some point during the sales process, a demonstration will go wrong. Many causes can lead to such failures, of course. For a complex product, adequate time may simply not have been spent preparing the demonstration. It may also be that the technical depth of the sales force is not sufficient to present product demonstrations repeatedly without fail.

Virtualization can help in this area by making it much more likely that even demonstrations given by nontechnical presenters will appear polished and cover core product features without error.

For example, consider a complex product that requires the salesperson to configure network connectivity between two physical machines in order to set up a demonstration properly. With virtualization, all of the network settings and the linkages between the two machines can be captured by a combination of profile settings in the virtualization software, as well as configuration settings persisted by the operating systems that are installed on the individual virtual machines. Figure 6.3 shows a sample Virtual Network Editor that simplifies network configurations of this type.

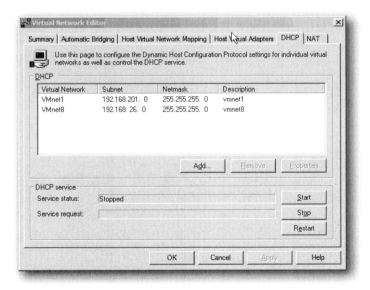

Figure 6.3   Virtual Network Editor Provides Simple Configuration Tools

In this case, the sales person simply launches the virtual machines in the appropriate order and then begins the demonstration. Further, with the creative use of batch files and execution routines and scripts provided by various virtualization vendors, demonstrations can be launched with a simple one-click operation.

Sales Engineers, Technical Marketing Engineers, and Developer Evangelists

In many companies, a dedicated individual, or team of individuals, is devoted to building demonstration content for customers. In many cases, this same group is responsible for delivering the demonstration content to the customer. Individuals who fill such roles are known at various companies by titles such as Developer Evangelist, Technical Marketing Engineer, and Sales Engineer.

For this role within a company, virtualization can provide a host of benefits. Some of these benefits include increased speed at which you can create and test demonstrations, as well as an increased number of demonstrations that can be easily created on pre-release software.

Creating Demonstrations at Lower Cost

Obviously, the amount of time employees spend doing any task affects the bottom line. Generally speaking, the quicker any group of employees can get the job done, the lower the cost of those activities. Virtualization makes it easy to create demonstrations without the need to provide sales engineers with a variety of hardware setups. Consider the example of company that primarily develops software to run on the Macintosh† OS X but also builds a portion of their product line to run on Microsoft Windows.

Typically, in this case, anyone building demonstrations would need access to both Macintosh hardware and hardware running Microsoft Windows. Virtualization makes it possible to easily utilize Microsoft's Virtual PC for Mac to run the Microsoft operating system in a virtualized environment on the Macintosh.

The savings on specialized hardware that comes about through virtualization can be significant for a large team of technical marketing engineers, sales engineers, or those with similar job roles and titles.

Testing Speed

In many cases, the team developing and conducting demonstrations in front of customers for a large company does not have the same dedicated Q/A resources that the development team has. The ability to utilize virtualization makes it much easier for a team of sales engineers to quickly test their demonstrations before showing them to an external audience, while also using less dedicated hardware. Sales engineers, for example, would have the ability to test complex networking scenarios or multi-machine interaction scenarios (such as a domain controller and multiple client machines), all on a single piece of hardware.

Demonstrating Pre-Release Software

Perhaps the greatest benefit that virtualization provides a team of sales engineers is that they can much more rapidly work with internal builds of a software product and build out demonstrations on those releases. It has recently become much more common, even for large software companies, to provide external releases of their software while it is still in development on a monthly basis.

For example, with Visual Studio 2005, Microsoft provided developer releases approximately every four to eight weeks throughout the approximately two-year development cycle for the product. This process continues with the development of the Windows Vista operating system, with releases occurring almost monthly. This type of release frequency demands that representatives of the company in contact with customers utilize current software pre-releases that many customers and potential customers might be using.

Previously, when products went through a lengthy development cycle and had widely separated and specific alpha, beta, and final release candidates, it was easier for a sales-engineering team to develop demonstrations that might have a shelf life of at least three months, and typically six months or more. This longevity meant that configuring a physical machine with a build of the software in development would cause one at worst to go through all of the manual configuration steps to reconfigure a demonstration machine every three months. With the more frequent release cycles by many software companies, however, sales engineering teams must make such changes far more frequently. Requiring a sales-engineering team to reload computers once a month or perhaps even more frequently than that can create an unacceptable level of time lost in front of customers.

Virtualization makes it possible for a dedicated subset of the team (or perhaps another team entirely who are not directly working with customers) to pre-build a variety of base images using the latest software releases and to distribute this software to the team at large. Enabling a team of sales engineers to function in this way means that those sales engineers are able to spend more time directly in front of the customers without wasting the entire team's time loading and configuring new software releases. In addition, as mentioned in Chapter 4, this same procedure of having a dedicated team of image builders could be utilized by the development team as well. Obviously, in this case, if both the development team and the sales-engineering team leveraged the same base images, a great amount of productivity could reclaimed from both teams.

Demonstrating Legacy Software

Another benefit virtualization offers to the sales-engineer team is the ability to quickly demonstrate legacy software or older software that is still in use by customers and/or being sold in conjunction with newer releases. An example of this situation is Microsoft continuing to sell Windows 2000 at the same time they are selling Windows XP licenses to customers. Another example might be showing interoperability with older, no-longer-standardized releases, such as Windows NT 4.0, in order to illustrate that a new product can still connect, communicate with, and share data with older releases of a product. Choosing an operating system default is extremely easy for all of the virtualization products, as shown in Figure 6.4 for the VMware Workstation product.

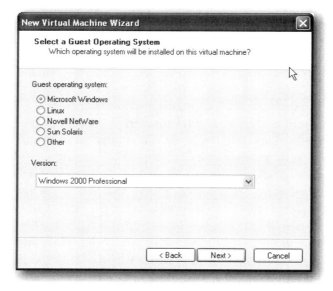

Figure 6.4   Choosing a Guest Operating System on VMware Workstation

In many cases, it may not be possible to install the older products on the same physical host machine as the newer releases, or the older products may exhibit instability problems if they are installed *after* the new release is already installed. This situation obviously presents a problem for the sales-engineering team, as they need to be able to limit the amount of hardware they are forced to configure and transport, particularly for edge scenarios. It is not hard to imagine a sales engineer who is going on out the road and needs to give 90 percent of demonstrations on the new product, 9 percent on the previous product, and another 1 percent for a single demonstration involving a legacy product the company produces. In that situation, the sales engineer has two choices without virtualization.

First, he or she may assume that the demonstration will run successfully while interacting with whatever production installation the customer has up and running. Even if this assumption proves correct, it is fraught with potential risk. One reason for this potential concern is that the customer may have customized their configuration of the software in such a way that limits or impairs the ability of the sales engineer to demonstrate the new product effectively. Worse yet, these changes may not all be documented, and they may not be fully understood by the sales engineer before he or she begins the demonstration, endangering the success of the demonstration.

The second choice open to a sales engineer who needs to support multiple environments on the road is to take additional hardware in the form of mobile platforms, or if the software requires server hardware, to ship a complete server platform. This cumbersome choice is no longer necessary if that sales engineer uses virtualization to solve the problem. With virtualization, sufficient disk space is all that is required to perform the installation of the product and the associated operating system, and the sales engineer can simply take one computer to perform all the demonstrations required on the trip. Shipping costs are reduced, and the headache of having to carry numerous machines through airports is avoided.

Evaluations

Evaluations are typically further along the sales cycle than demonstrations. Typically, the customer has been given the opportunity to work with the software for a period under the assumption that they will be so pleased with the ease of use of the software and the productivity benefits gained that they will purchase the product.

Many different individuals typically become involved at this stage. The effort may fan out to various parts of your organization, including the sales department, help desk, and sales engineers, as well as the various other departments, such as legal and accounting. Considering the amount of billable time being expended at this stage, it is important to consider the ramifications of a sales cycle that doesn't end with a sale of your product. Early in the sales cycle, it is easy to write off the lost effort, but by late in the cycle, your company will have expended a great deal of billable time on the customer in order to get them to buy your product. Being able to get them to the point of purchase is critical at this stage, in order to avoid losing the investment that you have already made.

Virtualization can help by giving you the ability to package up a series of servers, a single server product, or even a desktop product, in a single virtualized package that allows the customer to avoid any configuration and installation difficulties, which are common in any evaluation scenario. That increase in the likelihood of success in the customer's installation of the product can easily make the difference between a lost and a completed sale. If your product is of a sufficient price point, you can even suggest bundling in a virtualization vendor's product, so that the experience the customer has running the virtualized solution (with no installation and configuration headaches) is the same when they purchase and go into production.

In addition, if you choose to allow it, the customer can take the same collection of images and quickly and easily provide them to other members of the organization or to remote locations by simply copying them across an internal network for evaluation. Once the virtualized evaluation package arrives at the destination, there is limited need to determine what the remote facility has in terms of hardware and software, as long as they can run the virtualization client or server software that you have recommended and have appropriate resources in terms of RAM, disk space, and CPU resources to run the virtual machines.

Some concerns to keep in mind are that a company needs to analyze the performance impact of running a virtualized solution and accurately communicate the level of resources required on a host machine to run it. For example, it is likely that you will need to specify additional memory, and you may have to specify additional requirements, such as running virtual machines on dedicated hard disks, as well as specific CPU requirements.

One other consideration is that you should package up the virtual machines with as much documentation, quick-start material, and targeted training content as possible. If you offer the client the ability to migrate the virtual machines throughout their network as part of the evaluation process, you will need to ensure that a user who accesses the virtual machine has the appropriate context and necessary background information to have a successful experience using the software. Using a quick-start approach, where a single web page is loaded upon virtual machine boot up that points out key considerations, first steps, and links to resources in this case, is very beneficial.

Hosted Demonstrations

One other viable approach, especially with server-based virtualization products such as VMware's ESX and GSX server and Microsoft's Virtual Server product, is that you can also set up hosted demonstrations that can be accessed remotely. This technique retains all of the benefits of the previously outlined approaches, with the only significant requirement being access to a web connection in order to remotely connect with the machines running on the back-end server.

Assuming that you can find a reliable Internet connection for the demonstration, this scenario also provides the benefit of being able to leverage back-end hardware and have a team of sales engineers be able to maximize the resources of a server or collection of servers. That utilization of resources has financial benefits, relative to supplying each of them with a powerful enough mobile computer to run the virtual machines locally. On the other hand, risk does exist in terms of potential loss of connectivity during a demonstration. Finally, assuming that the demonstrations are well-documented, potential customers could be directed to utilize these servers directly as part of the product-evaluation process.

World-Wide Marketing

The ability to quickly set up a series of virtual machines for worldwide distribution via DVD or over the Internet makes the step of building out a series or even a library of demonstration content on virtual machines a critical step for a company working with a global market. In addition, virtualization makes it much easier to store and transport for given events a series of localized images that can be readily used in a given locale. A set of such virtual machines could be very valuable for a sales engineer who has a coverage area that extends across countries with various primary languages. In addition, server virtualization makes it easy to provide a library of remotely accessible images targeted at various locales and geographies that a remote presenter can access easily.

Ensuring Success

The key benefit of virtualization in the areas of product sales and marketing is that virtualization helps to prevent the failure of demonstrations. Virtualization also helps ensure that customers see a complete demonstration in the shortest amount of time with the greatest possible impact. By taking advantage of virtualization for hosted demonstrations and locale specific images, you can provide a better experience for potential customers.

In addition, virtualization makes allows you to take better advantage of in-house resources such as sales engineers by enabling them to focus more completely on customer interaction. The use of this technology provides support to sales engineers by reducing cumbersome manual setups, complicated live demonstration concerns at the customer's site, and other time-consuming endeavors that are inevitable without the use of virtual machines.

Developer and Partner Training

Typically, when developing complex software packages, it is helpful to develop training programs that align with the key concepts that users of the software need to know. For more complex software packages, such as development tools and infrastructure tools, it can be beneficial to have in-depth training that covers the product from end to end, in terms of its technical capabilities.

Instructor Led Training (ILT) can be a very costly proposition, however. Even when training can be done on the company's premises, it can still be costly to hire an outside trainer and provide curriculum.

It is critical that customers attempting to use your product after purchase are able to overcome potential implementation barriers and/or known limitations of the product. Virtualization makes it easier to implement training solutions that help minimize the costs of standard ILT training and can even help minimize the costs of developing and delivering Online Training (OLT).

Training Setup

A typical consideration when putting together a training event is the amount of configuration that goes into setting up a typical classroom environment. Before looking at how virtualization can help, consider how a typical classroom is set up without virtualization.

Manual Install

For a very small training session, manual installation procedures may be used to set up the training environment. This scenario is obviously not optimal, by any means. For example, consider the amount of time to set up the following configuration on a typical desktop computer if done manually.

- Windows XP Professional (approximately 30 minutes)
- Office 2003 (10 to 20 minutes)
- Visual Studio 2005 (1 hour to 3 hours)

The total time to perform the installation above *per computer* is approximately two to four hours, depending on the performance characteristics of the hardware onto which the software is being loaded. These figures do not include potential lag due to each machine waiting for manual input at various stages of the install process.

Of course, options other than a manual install are typically employed, such as those discussed below.

Answer Files

Sometimes companies set up a series of answer files that automatically fill in the values required during setup of given software applications, such as product keys, default user names, network settings, partition sizes, and a variety of other possible inputs. While this technique does alleviate the need to enter values manually, it does not limit, in any significant way, the amount of time it takes to set up a training environment.

Imaging

Many companies invest heavily in tools such as Symantec's Ghost software that allow an individual to create a complete software clone of a computer and persist it to a single file. While these images can be deployed, it is important to consider that these images are not immediately bootable, and they take some time to create. To create a software image using a tool such as Symantec's Ghost product for an 8-gigabyte partition might take approximately 20 to 30 minutes. Deploying this image takes approximately 20 to 30 minutes more.

In addition, the process of deploying the image requires that a given partition on the host computer is completely replaced with the persisted image. This is in significant contrast to the use of virtualization, where the host machine is not affected except for the use of additional disk space to store the virtual machines.

The software-image model also typically renders the host machine inaccessible while the image is being reloaded or when an image is being made. This characteristic is also in contrast to a virtualization scenario, where the host machine is accessible both when building an image and when copying new images to the machine.

This inaccessibility may not be a problem in some training environments, where a classroom is used for a single purpose or course each day. In many cases, however, training centers, colleges, and other schools need to keep classrooms in use throughout the day. In these cases, it would not be possible, for example, to quickly switch from a network administration class to a class on Microsoft Office essentials in a timely enough fashion using imaging to allow the classes to be scheduled nearly back-to-back, as would be typical on a college campus. With virtualization, an educational institution can easily switch a classroom from one environment to another without the need for the excessive downtime associated with a solution based on imaging.

Removable or Portable Hard Drives

Another solution that is commonly attempted for training setup is the use of portable or removable hard drives. This model does allow the machine to be "reloaded" with new software simply by replacing a drive but it comes at the cost of having a hard drive that matches each classroom setup. With virtualization you can simply store multiple virtual machines on a single drive.

How Virtualization Changes Things

Virtualization makes it possible to easily configure and set up training rooms, much as for the demonstrations discussed above. This capability means that a training room can be switched easily from one environment to the other, simply by powering up another virtual machine on the same computer, allowing more classes to be held in a given classroom and taking better advantage of resources.

Since a computer lab or training center represents a very substantial hardware expenditure, making efficient use of that hardware throughout the day with limited lag is critical. For example, the average cost of a classroom setup for a 25-person classroom would be approximately USD 50,000 for the computer equipment alone, including desktop computers, associated peripherals, and computer monitors. This cost does not include additional expensive infrastructure, such as video-projection systems and other elements to support the training environment. Making sure that each training room is used frequently is an important consideration, to make appropriate use of the initial cost outlay to outfit the classroom.

It is even possible to save the state of individual student sessions, giving each participant his or her own dedicated virtual machine. Considering the increasingly large hard drives provided with even moderate desktop machines, it would be very easy to store numerous images on a given desktop hard drive for each student who uses them throughout the day. These files could be secured from access by other students using standard Windows file-system permissions.

Server-based virtualization provides for even more significant cost savings. Students can have an experience identical to that found by using a workstation machine, but the company has the flexibility of supplying that experience through dedicated server hardware that can be fully utilized and more easily scaled, configured, and maintained than a large collection of desktop computers.

Finally, in corporate training environments where the training occurs once a week or is a weekend course, it is also possible with virtualization (assuming software licensing considerations are met) to allow the students to quickly burn to DVD and take home their virtual machine(s) for the week. This capability would allow them to quickly and easily work on the exact environment that was provided by the corporate training environment and then use the same images when class begins again.

Training on Old Products

In many cases, companies need to retain legacy systems. These same companies must also sometimes train new employees to operate these legacy systems. As mentioned previously in this chapter, virtualization can make it easier to create a solution that runs on legacy software for demonstration purposes. For training purposes, this capability can be even more critical, as the company may rely on previously purchased software running on operating systems, databases, and so on that no longer have vendor support.

In these cases, it might be difficult to acquire hardware on which the software will install. That limitation may be particularly salient if multiple machines are required to train a new series of employees to interface with customers about the software from a customer-support standpoint. Virtualization can make the need to find such legacy hardware irrelevant, making it easier for the company to train its support staff for the software product.

Student Behavior and Experience

It is notoriously difficult to determine the degree of technical competency among a given group of students prior to the start of a training class. This shortcoming can affect the training environment in unexpected ways. In the case of a product that has security configuration requirements that might lock out the machine if done incorrectly (which is common in some products), it is important to have an environment that can be easily reset to a predefined state.

While imaging would help alleviate this concern, most students would be dissatisfied waiting 20 to 30 minutes for a machine to reload, even if the mistake was their fault. This shortcoming would be all the more pronounced if re-imaging were required multiple times during a single class session.

In these types of situations, virtualization can be an obvious choice. Through the use of backup images, snapshots, undo files, and other options, virtualization software can protect students from inadvertent errors that might significantly affect the stability or accessibility of their computers.

Hosted Experiences

One example of significant cost savings comes about as part of the utilization of hosted experiences. Hosted experiences give the software-development company the ability to provide customers using server-based virtualization a classroom style experience over the web. Hosted experiences allow the company to provide multiple machine configurations and complex environments with full networking support without the hassle of local configuration and maintenance. A discussion of one such scenario follows in a later section of this chapter.

Power Considerations

An additional consideration as computer hardware has become more power-hungry is that training rooms can generate a significant cost to an organization in power consumption alone. For many of the same reasons that an organization might choose to consolidate its data center into a more limited set of physical machines by leveraging virtualization technology, a group chartered with training a large number of partners and customers might see similar benefits in terms of cost savings. Being able to use a server-based virtualization solution for a training environment can save significantly on power-consumption costs, as the organization has the ability to host an entire set of student virtual machines on a smaller set of computers than would have been the case if physical machines had been used for each student.

Staffing and Administration

Training is typically at best a break-even business for most software development companies, and for many, it represents a loss. It is nevertheless necessary, in order to ensure continued software sales and the continued successful utilization of the software from current customers. Virtualization also helps software companies minimize costs in staffing and administration associated with training efforts.

Staffing

The typical training environment is set up by a team of individuals responsible for maintaining the configuration of training machines, ensuring that they are loaded with the proper software from day to day, ensuring that changes users might have made to the machines are set back to an appropriate baseline for training, and various other tasks. With virtualization, the training environment can be more easily maintained. Whether a desktop virtualization or server virtualization scenario is utilized, staffing levels can be typically reduced, due to the flexibility that virtualization provides in terms of speedier training room setups that then do not require as many hours per training event to initialize and configure prior to the use of virtualization technologies. For a large company that frequently provides training on its software to customers, this benefit can become quite substantial over time.

Configuration, Administration, and Hardware

You will have fewer overall administration headaches when you use virtualization for a training environment. By not having to administer what might amount to hundreds of computers in a large training organization, and limiting the environment to just a handful of key servers from which students run their virtual machines, you can realize significant savings.

Typically, when a new software release is rolled out, it has higher hardware requirements than its predecessor. This characteristic typically puts a strain on the training organization, as they are compelled to upgrade all of the training machines to a given baseline. To take one recent example, when Microsoft released Windows XP, many training centers were still operating machines configured with 64 to 128 megabytes of memory in their classrooms. In order to meet adequate performance goals, many of these machines were upgraded to 256 megabytes. The core matter to consider is that this these upgrades had to be performed on *every machine*. If a server virtualization scenario had been used, a much smaller number of machines would have required an upgrade. This scenario would have saved significantly on the time required to open each computer, install the new memory, and verify that it was working correctly. It also most likely would have saved money, due to the ability to maximize the use of the memory available on the server machines supporting a virtualized classroom scenario.

Software Delivery

One interesting ramification of virtualization that is just beginning to be explored is the use of virtualization software and virtual machines for the deployment of software as a packaged solution. While software is typically sold in a state that can be run in a virtualized environment, it is typically not available for sale in a pre-packaged virtual machine.

VMDrive

The notion of selling software pre-configured in a virtual machine has begun to emerge, however. For example a visit to the web site www.vmdrive.com, shown in Figure 6.5, illustrates this business model in action.

Figure 6.5   The VMDrive Web Site Home Page

VMDrive provides packaged and pre-built virtual machines for VMware and Microsoft virtualization software for ESX Server, GSX Server, Workstation, Virtual Server 2005, and Virtual PC 2004.

VMDrive also goes to the level of providing pre-packaged software solutions such as open source CRM software and other types of applications simply available for download.

What this Modality Means for Software Vendors

The reality is that virtualization has some serious impact on distribution solutions and has a large effect on the bottom line if you use proprietary software that requires licenses to use it. One of the more significant drawbacks to developing on the Linux platform is that it is harder to configure than competing platforms. The availability of pre-built virtual machines, pre-loaded with open-source software and already configured for use, lessens the impact of this argument. What this potential trend means for software developers remains to be seen, but it is an area worth watching.

Software developers should also look for ways to deploy their software in a virtualized format, so that they can potentially reach out to audiences who might be expecting this type of delivery model from more vendors in the future.

Deploying Fully Integrated Systems of Virtual Machines

Another important consideration stems from the fact that with virtual machine technology, you can quickly and easily deploy (as mentioned previously) an entire suite of machines already preconfigured to interact with one another on a host machine. This means that for some complex configurations, this may become one of the standard methods of delivery with a client-tier virtual machine, a middle-tier virtual machine, and a back-end virtual machine, all delivered simultaneously by the same software vendor, as a software package that can be run with virtualization software.

Some Examples

This section highlights some high-profile use cases of virtualization technology by major companies. These use cases provide additional concrete examples of how virtualization can be used for marketing, selling, or educating users about a packaged software product.

VMware Case Study

One of the more interesting case studies for the use of virtualization and the packaging of software is VMware themselves. Somewhat recently on VMware's VMware Technology Network (VMTN), shown in Figure 6.6, VMware began providing fully configured virtual machines for customers to download.

Figure 6.6   VMware's VMware Technology Network

While it is worth noting that VMware has an obvious stake in the use of virtual machines as the core part of a distributed solution, they have taken some great strides in providing complete solutions on their site. For example, from the VMware site, you can download the following:

- SUSE[†] Linux Enterprise Server and Novell[†] Linux Desktop
- Red Hat[†] Enterprise Linux
- IBM[†] Workplace Services Express pre-installed on Red Hat Linux
- BEA WebLogic[†] Platform pre-installed on Red Hat Linux
- mySQL pre-installed on SUSE Linux
- Oracle[†] Database 10*g*

Once you have gone through the free registration process, you can download packages that range in size from 500 megabytes (MB) to about 2 GB. After downloading, the installation process consists of pointing a tool such as VMware Player or one of the other VMware tools at the image and booting it.

The implications of this modality are clear, in that no Microsoft software can be delivered through this method. Considering Microsoft's current dominance in the markets for operating system and other applications, this is an interesting area to watch over the long term.

Microsoft

While Microsoft has some obvious challenges to delivering their software in a virtualized scenario due to licensing concerns, it is important to note the areas where they have invested heavily in virtualization.

Hosted Experiences

Microsoft has invested heavily through the years in hosted experiences. For a number of years now, both partners and the general developer community have been able to benefit via test drives and hosted experiences. One example is the recent Visual Studio 2005 launch.

Microsoft utilized Virtual Labs, shown in Figure 6.7, to allow potential customers or a customer who had recently acquired the product to learn about features in an online-hosted virtualized environment.

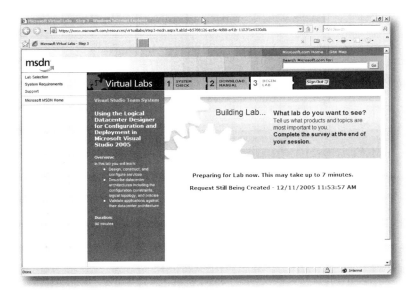

Figure 6.7   Microsoft Virtual Labs

Using this approach for early customer engagement gives Microsoft the ability to let users test drive their software early in the development cycle.

Early Software Releases

One interesting recent trend with Microsoft is the use of virtualization technology to enable external developers to come up to speed quickly with a new technology. One good example of this is the Visual Studio Team Suite and the associated Team Foundation Server product.

In order to understand the discussion, a small amount of context is in order about two products. Visual Studio Team Suite is an enhanced version of the Visual Studio product for .NET developers. Visual Studio Team Suite has enhanced functionality, such as source-code control and reporting when it is integrated with the back-end Team Foundation Server product.

While Visual Studio Team Suite has an install process that is very similar to that of its predecessor's, the back-end server Team Foundation Server has a fairly complicated setup routine. For example, the following core components are required to set up a Team Foundation Server:

- Windows Server 2003
- Internet Information Services 6.0, a web server that comes with Windows Server 2003
- Windows SharePoint Services 2.0 with SP2
- SQL Server 2005 Database Server
- Various settings to configure traffic through firewalls

One should not assume that a developer, architect, or upper-level manager on the development side of a company necessarily has the IT skills to install this software successfully. Moreover, the installation guide runs approximately 40 pages for all of this functionality, and the install process takes approximately three to four hours to complete, even on reasonably new hardware.

Microsoft faces a significant problem in terms of users being able to quickly get up to speed and see Team Foundation Server's features and benefits, because of the complexity of successfully installing the product. This issue is difficult to mitigate, due to the potential gap between the knowledge base of an average developer and the IT knowledge required to install software packages like SQL Server 2005, Windows SharePoint Services, and Windows Server 2003.

Microsoft used an elegant solution to ensure that developers were able to get moving productively with the product without the need to go through a lengthy install process. After the beta 2 release of Team Foundation Server, Microsoft began to release virtual machines that were preconfigured to run Team Foundation Server. They have continued that process since that time, with major releases of the Team Foundation Server product being associated with a time-limited version of Team Foundation Server installed.

For Microsoft, this has been a significant success that has made it much easier for developers, architects, and development managers to quickly see the benefits provided by Team Foundation Server and Visual Studio Team Suite in tandem. Those benefits might otherwise have been obscured through incorrectly configured or failed installs of Team Foundation Server.

Training Experiences

Microsoft has also invested heavily in the use of virtualization for the training part of their partner program. Microsoft uses a technology developed by the company Granite Pillar that allows partners as well as other individuals through their e-learning initiative to easily access fully integrated solutions.

The console shown in Figure 6.8 allows training content to be presented on the left-hand side while giving students and customers the ability to quickly and easily navigate a fully functioning version of a product running as a virtual machine.

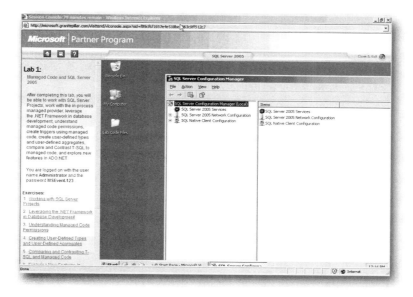

Figure 6.8   Virtualization Technology in Microsoft Partner Training

Using this model allows potential customers and current customers to easily interact with software over the web at the pre-purchase stage of a sales engagement. Another benefit of this technology is that it readily allows the user to use a multiple-machine configuration as part of the training content.

Microsoft Learning, a division of Microsoft that produces training courses for outside customers, has recently developed entire training courses that it delivers on a back-end Virtual Server infrastructure, to allow for easy initialization, setup, and reset of training courses between student sessions.

Conclusion

In this chapter, you have seen various ways that virtualization technology can provide support to a company in marketing software, by producing demonstrations more reliably and delivering them with greater impact. You have also seen the benefit that virtualization provides in terms of making better use of the time of key personnel who work directly with customers such as sales engineers. Lastly, the impact in terms of customer training initiatives has also been made clear.

The next chapter provides more discussion on the impact for more inward-facing members of the software development company, including testers, developers, architects, and others within the pure development part of the software organization.

Chapter 7

Current Limitations of Virtualization

Computers can figure out all kinds of problems, except the things in the world that just don't add up.

—James Magary

While virtualization provides enormous benefits, a running theme throughout this book, it is not a panacea for all development and IT-related issues. In certain environments virtualization has drawbacks; and in others, it is simply not a feasible solution. This chapter explores some of the cases where virtualization is not a good fit and where you may need to look elsewhere for a resolution until virtualization technologies cover more ground.

The ability to virtualize a machine is great for underutilized hardware in both IT and development environments. Being able to quickly switch between operating systems, revisions, and specialized configurations is a powerful tool, but unfortunately not all of the host machine's hardware is emulated and, therefore, available for the guest machines to utilize.

Applications that are CPU intensive are not always suitable candidates for virtualized hardware either, although this should change in the future with increased support for multi-core and multiprocessor architectures. Dedicating one or more processors or cores to a given virtual machine would be suitable for many applications, although any given CPU that is 100-percent utilized on a guest machine is still going to have fewer cycles than one that is 100-percent utilized on a stand-alone machine. The ability to apply more processing power to the challenge of emulating high-end graphic cards due to the VMM overhead and other types of devices discussed in this chapter is one way that emulation and other problems will be solved in the near future.

However, these are just some of the considerations. The rest of this chapter will address the limitations of today's virtualization solutions in the areas of advanced processor support, mobile applications, graphic intensive simulations, and others.

Advanced Processor Support

Most software assumes that a CPU and its full resources are always available. Support for 32-bit versus 64-bit architectures are managed by the compiler and are of little interest to many developers. If a processor has more than one core, or if a motherboard incorporates more than one CPU, the application may or may not take advantage of it. Also if the CPU supports unique instructions such as graphics, the software assumes these capabilities will be present if they are to be leveraged.

For example, 64-bit support is a more recent addition to some virtualization products so many may not fully meet your needs due to the limited support in this area if you are working with 64-bit applications or developing a solution that requires 64-bit support. Some virtualization products will run only on 64-bit hardware if the underlying host operating system is a 32-bit version. In essence, this is taking away the benefits of 64-bit power.

As with the other limitations, vendors are aggressively working to reduce or remove the barriers.

Mobile Applications

The process of developing applications for mobile environments places a variety of challenges on a virtualized solution. For one thing, neither the battery nor the wireless network is currently virtualized in any solution today. In addition other types of networking support that are available via Bluetooth connections or the like are also not virtualized. In the following sections you'll see how these limitations can constrain your ability to use virtualization in mobile development scenarios as you are unable to test for low battery conditions and similar circumstances that you might want to detect if the software was running on an actual host machine.

Battery Life and Responding to Power Related Events

Of increasing concern to hardware and software manufacturers, but unfortunately ignored by many software developers, is the need to minimize battery use. One of the reasons that software developers are apt to sidestep this issue is that very few pervasive and publicly available tools exist for them to use to simulate, emulate, or virtualize a battery.

Compounding this problem is the fact that even if the developer is using a mobile workstation as a development platform that has a battery, access to the battery in the virtual machine is unavailable because the battery of the host platform is not virtualized.

With sales of mobile platforms beginning to outstrip those of desktop platforms, an inability to model battery life appropriately in a virtual machine will continue to be a serious hindrance to application developers, testers, and evaluators of software until an appropriate solution is devised.

Wireless Connectivity and Roaming Networks

One typical scenario for a mobile application is its use on the move while connected to various access points. Virtualization is suited for many network connectivity scenarios as discussed previously but for the ones outlined in the following sections, such as Wi-Fi[†] access and network roaming, it is not as tailored a solution as a user, developer, or IT administrator might prefer.

Wireless Connectivity

Being able to connect to a network wirelessly to gain access to e-mail and the Internet has quickly become ubiquitous. Many business travelers expect to find pervasive Internet access wherever they may go. However achieving a virtualized solution that provides wireless connectivity requires the use of the host's networking stack. This means that while the host machine can connect to an outside network through the use of its wireless connection, the virtual machine must connect through the virtual non-wireless network card that is emulated in the virtual machine. Figure 7.1 illustrates the way in which a virtual machine has to utilize the host machine's networking card in order to connect to a wireless card.

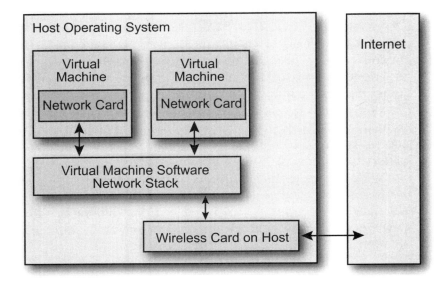

Figure 7.1   Accessing a Host Machine's Wireless Card from a Virtual Machine

This is an adequate scenario for many uses, but it loses its usefulness if a developer is designing software for a wireless card or if a tester is verifying the functionality of a wireless toolset. It is also not as useful for a developer who is attempting to mimic the fluctuations in connectivity that can result from working on a wireless connection. However these fluctuations can be mitigated in part by some of the tools discussed in the software development section of the book. Regardless of the potential workarounds, there are no solutions at the moment that provide direct emulation of a wireless card in a virtual machine.

Roaming Networks

Being able to move seamlessly from one wireless network to another whether the technology is Wi-Fi, Bluetooth[†], or WiMAX is no longer a dream in the distant future but one that is coming closer to reality. Unfortunately, current virtualization solutions do not help if you want to test or demonstrate how an application performs as it moves between, say, a WiMAX network to a cellular network, down to a Bluetooth network, and then back again as the user roams through a geographic area with their device. Virtualization products today do not virtualize devices such as Bluetooth devices or cellular-based PCMCIA cards that provide Internet access.

In order to develop, test, or demonstrate applications that need to respond to these types of conditions, you must configure network settings that attempt to emulate the resultant network settings in terms of total bandwidth, latency, and shape of network traffic, which is possible with some virtualization products. However it is not possible to actually work with the application as if it were interacting with an actual Bluetooth, cellular, or WiMAX device inside the virtual machine because the vendors do not virtualize these types of devices.

Screen Size and Form Factor Issues

Another significant concern is the use of virtualization when it comes to testing devices with various form factors. Right now some of the standard form factors are cell phones, Pocket PC-style or Palm-style devices, notebooks of all variations, such as sub or desktop replacement, tablet PCs, and desktop machines. The usual assumption is that, as has happened in the past, various form factors will appear that bridge the gap between these devices and blur the distinctions that exist today.

Beyond some rudimentary support for changing desktop resolution, today's virtual machines are not effective at changing resolution dynamically to odd screen sizes or widths. Nor are they good at emulating an environment that has a variety of soft buttons. One exception is custom software or hardware vendor-supplied emulators such as the Pocket PC emulator that would simply run inside the virtual machine itself as part of a development environment. Therefore if you are building, deploying, or using applications that require you to work with odd and nonstandard displays, existing virtualization solutions will provide only incremental and perhaps no direct benefit.

Graphic-intensive Visualizations

No fully supported virtualization solution today allows for the use of graphic-intensive applications in a virtual machine. Primarily this is due to the most recent history of virtualization products being server side solutions where high end graphics were not a primary consideration. Games and graphic simulations or applications are not appropriate types of applications to run mainly because the graphics cards that are presently emulated for virtual machines have limited support. As

Chapters 1 and 2 pointed out, when it comes to graphics cards the current level of device emulation equates roughly to a graphics card that was available on a mainline desktop system in the late 1990s. This means that 3D rendering applications, 3D intensive games, 3D intensive simulations, and other software that requires a dedicated graphics processing unit will run *extremely* poorly and in many cases will crash or even fail to execute due to the poor performance of the emulated graphics CPU and the limited available video memory in the virtual machine. Currently, experimental support is available for Direct3D and graphics intensive applications in the VMware Workstation product.

Digitizers and Touch Screens

While still only a minor segment of the mobile market, tablet PCs and devices with touch screens and pen input are becoming more popular and the market is growing. Unfortunately current virtualization solutions do not offer any support in the areas of tablet PC ink input, digitizers, or touch screens. This means that you cannot develop, test, or evaluate these types of applications in any meaningful way using a virtualized environment.

Even if you mimic the mouse for some input and load an operating system, such as the Tablet PC operating system from Microsoft, into a virtual machine you still do not have the ability to use the full functionality available to tablet PCs in terms of ink input. Additionally, none of the mainstream virtualization products from Microsoft, VMware, or XenSource emulates a device that supports a touch screen digitizer.

It is unlikely that the major virtualization vendors will directly support these types of devices in the near term.

USB Devices

Support for USB at this time is either limited or nonexistent depending on the virtualization vendor. VMware, as mentioned in Chapter 2, does have some limited USB support as does Xen, whereas Microsoft has no USB support in its current product offerings.

The virtualization packages available today do not guarantee the same amount of compatibility with existing USB devices as you would expect from a host machine. This may mean that while a VMware virtual machine, for example, will detect a connected standard keyboard and mouse, it might not detect or even recognize a biometric fingerprint scanner.

This can also be a large limitation when it comes to USB dongle support for authentication as is common in some products. In cases like this where a server product such as Virtual Server or ESX does not support USB devices but the application software you are trying to install requires USB-based authentication using a dongle you will be unable to evaluate a solution or deploy a solution such as this on virtual machines.

Security Devices

Aligned with the previous discussion the current virtualization software available today does not detect most if not all physical security devices. One such example is a Tablet PC computer with an integrated fingerprint reader. At this point in time the only way to test an application that combines both fingerprint authorization and digital ink would be with physical hardware.

Virtual Machine Cataloging and Searching

If virtual machines proliferate as a delivery mechanism for software solutions and become more prevalent in IT scenarios, it will be critical to ensure that a given virtual machines' contents be easily cataloged and indexed. The toolsets of the current vendors have limited capability to catalog virtual machines and to search their contents without booting them directly. This leaves it up to the organization utilizing the virtual machine technology to define a manual process of cataloging a virtual machine and specifying what is installed on each machine.

Most indexing and search products look to the files present on a host machine alone as the key indicator of what needs to be indexed. These tools do not integrate well with running virtual machines nor do they allow the contents of virtual machines whose state is persisted to be indexed and catalogued.

Currently great effort is being expended to utilize virtual machines as a hardware or software model, but their ultimate viability may be limited if they cannot be indexed and hence searched as efficiently as the associated host computer. On a brighter note, tools already exist today that allow files to be loaded and unloaded into virtual machines that are not running at the time the operation is commenced. These types of tools may form the foundation of tools that can access a virtual machine's contents directly whether it is running or not and index and then catalog the contents for end user searches.

Balancing Utilization of Resources

While solutions exist at the server level, very few tools exist at the desktop level to guide the end user in allocating resources effectively across the virtual machines they are running. Power users of operating systems are somewhat accustomed to looking at memory utilization and CPU utilization for their applications and determining which one is taking away the most resources. However, the tools they use on a host operating system do not easily extend to help the end user in a similar way. Essentially current operating system tools force the end user to manage not only the balance of resources between virtual machines and the host machine but to then use the same tools inside each virtual machine to balance resource allocation inside each virtual machine. For desktop scenarios where a powerful workstation is utilized to run multiple virtual machines at the same time on a daily basis this need to manually tweak performance characteristics limits the use of today's virtualization tools.

Compile and Link Time

When developing and testing applications in a virtualized environment you'll need to consider the amount of time required to support compiling the application. If compile times are already high and are pressing the limits of what the company or a developer can afford, the overhead involved in virtualization will simply slow the processing down further. This performance limitation is more present with the desktop virtualization products but is still around to some degree with the server-based products.

Licensing

One of the largest limitations of virtualization software is in the area of licensing. While this has been discussed in context in other portions of the book it is important to examine licensing from an overall limitation standpoint although the current situation is very much in flux.

For products released by major vendors such as Microsoft, Oracle, IBM, and others you must read the licensing agreement very carefully to determine whether virtualizing a product you are using or developing affects your current software license agreements. What follows is a representative sampling of what one vendor, Microsoft in this case, has recently said about licensing at the time this was written. This information is to be used only as a general guide; any specific information about your licensing arrangement with a given vendor should always be extracted directly from the licensing agreements you have agreed to.

Until recently Microsoft's policy stated that each individual virtual machine in use required an equivalent license. For example, to run two Windows XP virtual machines on a host machine that is also running Windows XP meant you had to pay for three Windows XP licenses—one for each unique instance of Windows XP. Until recently it has been unclear whether this applied only to running virtual machines or all machines for which you had installed Windows XP. This issue was not commonly raised when Windows XP or another operating system from Microsoft was installed on physical hardware in the past. However the possibility to create literally tens or hundreds of images of XP on a single disk raises important licensing issues.

Microsoft recently released a document that describes the changes to licensing as it relates to virtualization. Here are some of the highlights:

- Licensing by running image. This means that you can store as many images as you want but pay for only the licenses of the maximum number of virtual machines that are active and launched at one time.

- The ability to move licenses from server to server as a virtual machine migrates from one server to another.

- More flexibility with other server products, such as SQL Server and BizTalk, in that these products will now be licensed by the *virtual* processors in use and not by just the number of physical processors that happen to be present on the machine on which these products are installed.

- With the Enterprise Edition of Windows Server 2003 R2 customers are able to run four virtual instances of the Windows Server 2003 product without additional expenditure for licenses.

Microsoft has established this licensing arrangement with Windows Server 2003 but has not yet formally extended it to legacy operating systems or current operating systems such as Windows XP. Also these arrangements apply to running Windows Server 2003 inside the VMware products as well.

But again this is just an example; it is important to review the current text of any license agreement you currently have with a software vendor to ensure that you are appropriately using licenses through virtualization.

Licensing arrangements are complex at the best of times for software and virtualization is bound—at least in the short term—to make that confusion even more pronounced regardless of which vendor you acquire a solution from.

Product Activation

Many products, ranging from Microsoft operating system products to other off-the-shelf commercial products, require some type of activation prior to being utilized and this holds true in the virtualization world as well. However, it is not possible to transfer the activation from on virtual machine to another even if one is about to be deleted and removed from the system permanently. Overall, this limitation is relatively minor when compared to others discussed in this chapter.

Conclusion

As previous chapters illustrated, virtualization provides a host of significant use cases across software development and IT scenarios. However significant limitations remain in today's solutions and these have to be understood in order to ensure that virtualization technologies are not assumed to be a panacea for all IT and software development issues that exist today.

The concluding chapter of this book takes a look forward into the future to see how some of these limitations might be addressed. It also provides a glimpse at future enhancements and usage models that might be available within the next ten years.

Chapter **8**

Resource Utilization and Flexibility

Less is more.

—Mies van der Rohe

While virtualization technology has been around for decades on IBM mainframes, its relatively recent appearance on Intel® processors has moved virtualization into the spotlight, especially as more and more usages are devised that provide significant business value for the IT department. Virtualization is already transforming the way many IT organizations provision and manage their systems and applications. For example, using a platform that is capable of taking advantage of Intel Virtualization Technology, IT professionals can consolidate multiple operating systems and applications onto a single server, thereby reducing the number of servers required, simplifying IT infrastructure, and reducing costs. Virtualization also increases the IT department's ability to adapt to change. The mobility of virtual machines across host platforms forms the basis for many usage scenarios that demonstrate the flexibility that virtualization brings, which includes the ability to easily adapt to shifting workload requirements, smoothly roll out software updates and services, and improve interoperability with legacy software. These capabilities are delivering substantial value to businesses today; and adoption will increase dramatically over the next few years as virtualization technology is delivered in Intel platforms and adopted by virtual machine software vendors, and as new usages are realized.[1]

This chapter presents a few of the ways that IT professionals can benefit from applying virtualization to practical problems they face; in particular, how to save money without decreasing services, while at the same time trying to increase flexibility and responsiveness to customers.

Resource Utilization

Before virtualization, a machine's operating system was bound directly to the underlying physical hardware. The operating system managed access to the physical hardware, including the processor, memory, and other physical resources. In fact, many operating systems include a hardware abstraction layer that encapsulates much of the underlying hardware and provides a logical abstraction layer to the rest of the operating system. This binding of the operating system and hardware has an important consequence: a hardware platform can host only a single operating system at a time. It isn't possible to have two operating systems cooperate to share the underlying resources; each operating system is written to "own" and manage the physical hardware by itself, as Figure 8.1 shows.

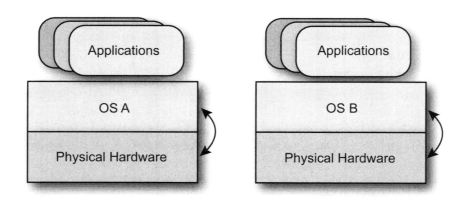

Figure 8.1   Operating Systems "Bound" to Underlying Hardware

---

[1] According to estimates from IDC, 8 percent of servers shipped with provisioning and virtualization features in 2003, and the number will grow to 40 percent in 2007.

The virtual machine monitor (VMM) provides a *virtual* hardware platform to the operating system, removing the dependency of the operating system on the underlying physical hardware. Virtualization of hardware resources therefore results in the ability to host multiple operating systems simultaneously on a single platform, which forms the basis for the following two usage scenarios.

Consolidating Servers

Without the ability to run multiple operating systems simultaneously on the same platform, the IT manager's deployment choices are constrained. For example, if one application requires operating system A and another application requires operating system B (or a different version of the same operating system), both applications must run on separate platforms, each with the appropriate operating system. This impedes the IT manager's ability to freely load-balance resources and to ensure that hardware resources are utilized to their fullest. Like packing using only large boxes, the choices that the IT manager must make under this constraint often result in underutilizing the available hardware resources; a server that has excess processing power available may not be utilized because an application that could run there requires a different operating system. Applications cannot be "packed" together as easily as one would like.

Astute data center managers, looking to capitalize on opportunities for more powerful, cost-effective data centers, have adopted virtualization as a way to increase server utilization. Instead of having many of the servers on, but idle and wasting computing cycles much of the time, data center managers have begun to provide the same level of service with less hardware, often dramatically reducing hardware acquisition and maintenance costs.

What were previously discrete physical servers are now virtual servers on a single virtualization-enabled host machine, as Figure 8.2 shows.

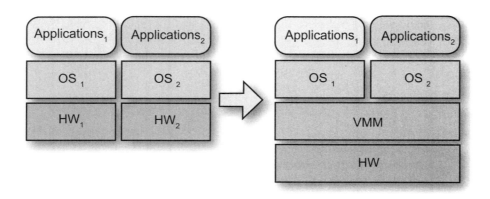

Figure 8.2   Workload Consolidation

Server consolidation also has secondary benefits, beyond a reduction in hardware costs, that help further reduce the total cost of ownership, including

- *Space Savings.* As fewer servers are required, less floor space is required to contain them.

- *Energy Savings.* Fewer servers consume less energy, generate less heat, and require less energy to cool.

- *Labor Savings.* Fewer servers require less administration. Companies typically assign approximately 7 mission critical servers to each administrator or 15 non-mission critical servers per administrator. Virtualization can double or triple that ratio so that a single administrator can handle 14 to 20 mission critical servers.

Consolidating applications onto a single platform to improve resource utilization is a strategy that you can apply to client computers as well. Although many applications are ported to multiple operating systems, the selection of an application is inextricably bound to the operating system it requires. Being able to freely select applications without regard for the operating system they require will level the playing field for applications and allow users to choose the best application for the task. The ability to run multiple operating systems simultaneously on a single host will open up new possibilities for productivity and experimentation.

Using virtualization to increase resource utilization is the strategy that IT departments are actively using today and it will continue to be one of virtualization's primary benefits, especially as computational power continues to increase. Figure 8.3 illustrates how virtualization results in fewer but more fully utilized physical resources.

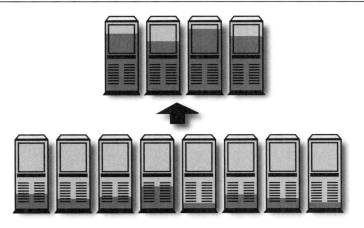

Figure 8.3   Increasing Resource Utilization

Multi-core processors will be able to run even more operating systems and tasks simultaneously, and the overhead required for each virtual machine will decrease as hardware support for virtualization is adopted by virtual machine software vendors.

Simplifying Server Management

Consolidating servers onto a smaller number of physical machines can simplify server management by reducing the number of machines to be monitored. However, it emphasizes the need for stable physical hardware; the physical hardware hosting multiple operating systems and applications becomes a single point of failure. If one of the physical machines has a hardware problem, or if it must be rebooted, it will affect many (virtual) servers and have a greater impact on availability of services than would otherwise be the case on separate physical servers. Therefore, the reliability of the physical servers and the ability for server administrators to monitor and control both the physical and virtual servers becomes even more important than before. Server management tools that provide monitoring and alerting capabilities are essential.

Fortunately, VMM vendors provide full-featured virtual infrastructure management solutions. VMware's VirtualCenter, for example, provides a central point of control for an organization's virtual computing resources. VirtualCenter allows an administrator to centrally manage hundreds of servers from a single management console. An administrator can monitor an individual virtual machine's usage of system resources using the list of virtual machines that VirtualCenter provides, shown in Figure 8.4.

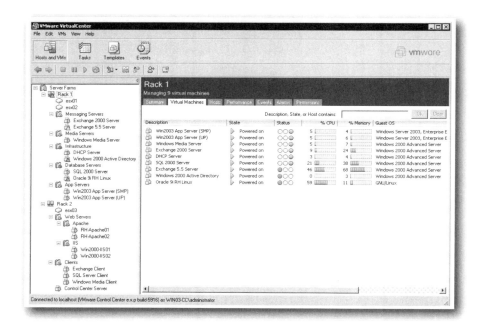

Figure 8.4   The VirtualCenter Management Console

The administrator can configure alarms and tasks based on events occurring on the virtual machine or according to a fixed schedule. Configuration and performance reports that VirtualCenter generate can help the administrator identify resource issues or potential hardware failures and can help guide further resource optimizations. With VirtualCenter, an administrator manages the virtual machines as a single pool of resources and can dynamically move virtual machines across distributed physical servers. Access control is managed globally across servers and virtual machines.

VMware's Virtual Infrastructure Software Development Kit (SDK) is another important capability that supports easier server management. Developers and administrators can use this SDK to programmatically invoke all functions of the VirtualCenter client, such as adjusting resource allocations for virtual machines or provisioning and balancing the server loads. The ability to programmatically control the functionality provided by the VirtualCenter facilitates the automation of key system administration tasks and the development of custom management applications. Using the SDK, administrators can automate tasks of their choice, either according to a pre-determined schedule or in response to events from the virtual machines. This flexibility exceeds what is possible with a physical server deployment.

In addition to the management solutions provided by the VMM vendors, traditional management tools already used in data centers are also becoming virtualization aware and are integrating with VMMs. As they incorporate the functionality provided by products like VirtualCenter, the traditional management consoles will be used to manage the virtual infrastructure as well.

As virtualization enters the computing mainstream, the improvements in manageability software and methodologies will ensure that using an increasing number of virtualized hosts will not trade a savings in hardware for system management complexity. Businesses will be able to use virtualization to build cost-effective, next-generation computing environments and optimized data centers.

Flexibly Managing Change

While the IT department can carefully determine the best configuration of virtual machines on physical servers, the IT environment doesn't remain static for very long. Customer needs change. Demand for services changes. New software with important security fixes must be deployed. Virtual machines can be run side by side (either different operating systems entirely, or different versions of the same operating system), moved from one physical machine to another, and "brought to life from suspended animation" by activating a previous snapshot. When used in conjunction with rapid software provisioning tools as described in the previous section, these features of virtualization can help the IT department to be responsive and flexible and adapt to changing requirements and meet customer needs with speed and agility.

Supporting Legacy Operating Systems

As time goes on, new operating system versions are released. Businesses often have commercial or internally developed software that is designed to run on older operating system versions. To maintain the continuity of the business, the IT department must keep these potentially unsupported and obsolete operating systems and applications up and running.

As already described, IT would like to use a consolidation strategy to reduce costs and perhaps move the applications to a new, more powerful server. However, although new hardware might provide sufficient power to run these older applications as well as more new applications; without virtualization, the legacy operating systems and applications can't be consolidated with newer applications that require new operating systems. Also, some applications are written to run in isolation on a server and cannot coexist with other applications on the same server because of security, compatibility, or data integrity issues. Porting the older programs to the new operating systems is a potential solution, but is usually not an option because of the costs associated with software development. Therefore, IT must use separate machines that are dedicated to running the older operating system and applications.

Virtualization resolves these issues by allowing the physical server to be logically partitioned into several virtual machines (VMs), each isolated from the others, which can then host legacy operating systems and applications side by side with new applications and operating systems. In this way, IT organizations have the flexibility to maintain older versions of operating systems without the burden of maintaining separate machines. It is easy to maintain support for older services indefinitely. With virtualization, IT can also provide an older application that expects a specific hardware platform with a virtualized version of the hardware it requires. Even as the application moves to new servers, the virtual hardware platform is maintained.

Figure 8.5 shows how different operating system versions can be maintained, side by side, using virtualization.

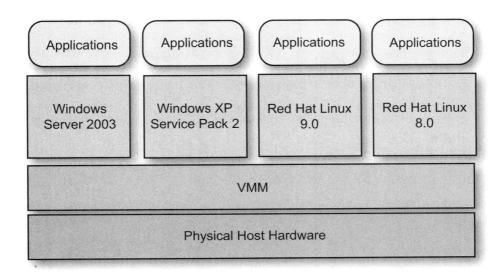

Figure 8.5   Hosting Multiple Operating Systems and Versions

Scaling Demand for Services

As businesses expand, their IT infrastructure must respond to changing end-user demands. Demand for some services will grow much faster than others, and a rapid, unanticipated spike in demand for a particular service can leave the IT department scrambling to respond.

Pre-virtualization, IT departments have typically adopted a simple scale-out server deployment model that has one application per server. As a new service is required, the department purchases the hardware to host the service, configures the server, and puts it into service. Or, as demand for an existing service increases, the IT department may buy a new, more powerful server and migrate the existing system to the new hardware.

While costly in terms of hardware, labor, and service downtime, this approach has been an effective way to handle rapidly expanding demand for services. However, as large numbers of these special purpose-built servers are added to data centers, the costs eventually become unacceptable. Single-application workloads simply do not scale well as demand increases. The cost due to underutilization and the corresponding increase in management complexity exceeds the benefits of the simple deployment model. For example, Gap Inc., a retail clothing company, traditionally added a new server each time they added a new project or application, an approach that ultimately resulted in Gap's IT group managing about 450 servers, with an utilization rate as low as 10 percent for more than 300 of the servers.

With a virtual infrastructure, the management of hardware is separated from the management of software. The hardware resources can be treated as a pool of processing, storage, and networking capability to be allocated to software services as needed. Administrators can allocate the virtual resources quickly in response to changing demand and are able to manage and optimize resources globally across the enterprise. Administrators can either increase the hardware resources, such as RAM, processors, or network bandwidth, available to a given virtual machine, or deploy new virtual machines.

Server consolidation and virtualization allowed Gap Inc. to consolidate one third of its existing servers to three, eight-way Intel Xeon® processor servers. They achieved a significant savings in equipment and system administration costs and, through virtualization, were able to boost uptime to greater than 99.99 percent. As this example shows, virtualization can help simplify IT planning and increase its responsiveness and ability to quickly and efficiently handle unanticipated changes in demand for service. Companies like Gap Inc. are reaping the benefits of consolidating servers and are enjoying the ability to easily scale services to demand by dynamically reallocating resources and shifting virtual machine workloads between servers.

Providing Pre-configured Services

IT customers typically specify the exact server configuration for an application. The IT group fulfills requests by putting together systems manually according to the customer specifications. This approach often produces many machines, each with its own custom configuration. Because each server may be configured to handle peak demand, much of the capacity is underutilized.

Because creating virtual machines is inexpensive relative to actually configuring physical servers, virtualization provides a way for the IT department to *anticipate* demand for services and to pre-configure virtual machines to have them ready to run or to further customize to match customer specifications. The IT department can establish a portfolio of pre-packaged, reusable services and move to an off-the-shelf model rather than build-to-order. Instead of specifying the hardware and the configuration needed for a business application, customers can choose from a variety of available services, each ready to deploy on a pre-configured virtual machine. As orders come in, a manager monitors the infrastructure for capacity planning and sourcing purposes.

Software Upgrades

Responding to the demands to improve performance, maintain security, or deliver new functionality requires the IT department to regularly update software. IT personnel must prepare servers, test them, and then replace or augment those that are currently deployed. If something goes wrong, personnel must be able to back up to the previous version and restore the servers to their original state. A physical machine approach means preparing separate machines, which requires additional hardware, or taking down the currently running servers to update them, which impacts availability. Restoring follows the same pattern.

Virtualization, on the other hand, facilitates the smooth transition of software without requiring additional hardware. Virtualization-capable platforms can run legacy and new operating systems concurrently. IT personnel can prepare and test new virtual machines on a development machine before deploying them on the server. Whether it's testing operating system patches, complex application deployments, or entirely new services, virtualization helps the updates to proceed smoothly. Then, if something goes wrong, it is easy to restore the image of a previous virtual machine. The following scenarios show how these advantages can be used for many kinds of software roll-outs.

Upgrading Server Operating Systems and Patches

Viruses and other attacks commonplace in today's networks and security problems can wreak havoc on an organization's computing infrastructure. Software vendors frequently release patches to address security flaws or fix other bugs, but to be effective the patches must be applied right away. Unfortunately, as the number of machines an administrator is responsible for increases, manually patching, upgrading, and maintaining operating system and application software simply doesn't scale well. In addition, having to patch or upgrade a critical server can also result in unacceptable system downtime. As a result, it is not unusual for servers to continue to run unpatched software long after a security exploit has been discovered and a software vendor has released a patch for it.

An upgrade strategy for servers that takes advantage of virtualization scales much better than the manual patching process. When faced with the task of implementing a security patch, administrators don't have to interrupt the availability of the hardware platforms; patching the operating systems in virtual machines is entirely a software operation. Virtual machines can be suspended, resumed, and migrated across physical platforms without interrupting service availability. The administrator can duplicate the existing virtual machines to be patched, apply the patch, and then test the result. Once the new images are ready, the administrator can transition to the new virtual machines. Using virtualization, administrators can perform operating system updates while preserving availability.

Transitioning to x86-based, 64-bit Operating Systems

There are 64-bit versions of operating systems available today that utilize Intel Extended Memory 64 Technology (Intel EM64T) to achieve higher levels of performance than is possible with 32-bit systems. 64-bit processors can process more data per clock cycle than their 32-bit counterparts and can access terabytes of physical and virtual memory, which benefits memory-intensive applications such as database, data mining, and scientific and engineering computing. A business that wants to gain the benefits of 64-bit performance and, at the same time, take advantage of the cost savings and flexibility provided by virtualization will require a 64-bit capable virtualization solution. Fortunately, vendors such as VMware have announced plans to bring virtualization to 64-bit extended platforms. For example, VMware's GSX Server 3.2 adds support for 64-bit host operating systems, and Workstation 5.5 introduces support for virtual machines with 64-bit guest operating systems.

Support for both 64-bit operating systems and 32-bit operating systems together on the same platform protects investments in existing operating systems and applications software while facilitating migration to 64-bit platforms. VMM support for 64-bit extensions will allow users to mix 32-bit and 64-bit operating system environments within the same system, as Figure 8.6 shows.

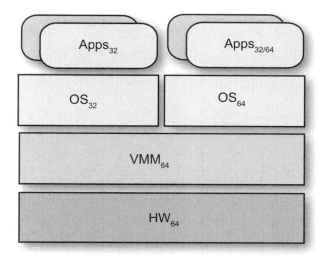

Figure 8.6   64-bit-capable Virtual Environment

64-bit-capable VMMs make it easy to consolidate existing 32-bit server workloads onto the latest x86-based 64-bit platforms. 64-bit operating systems can run older 32-bit applications alongside new 64-bit applications, while 32-bit operating systems can run 32-bit applications. Administrators have the control to use the 32-bit and 64-bit operating systems and applications that they choose. For example, administrators can decide to move workloads that don't benefit from 64-bit extensions directly to 32/64-bit platforms without any changes, while changing to 64-bit versions of those applications that benefit from 64-bit processors. VMMs provide the IT department even more flexibility and can help smooth the transition to new 64-bit platforms.

Deploying Applications with Advanced Compiler Optimizations

Advanced compiler optimizations are the key to realizing the performance benefits of 64-bit processors. The Intel C++ compiler, for example, has many sophisticated optimizations, including

- ■ *Automatic vectorization.* The compiler generates code such that a single processor instruction operates on multiple data items simultaneously.

■ *Automatic parallelization.* The compiler automatically parallelizes CPU-intensive sections so that at run-time the code uses multiple threads to execute the sections in parallel.

■ *Whole program optimization.* The compiler is able to analyze all modules in the program to perform optimizations across module boundaries.

■ *Profile-guided optimization.* The compiler further optimizes the code by using run-time feedback from previous runs of the program.

The availability of open source server software, like the Apache HTTP server, the MySQL† database, and others, makes it easy to experiment with compilation techniques to improve performance. Compiler optimizations such as those available with the Intel C++ compiler can be applied to server applications by recompiling the source code, potentially resulting in a large performance increase. For example, users who want to support multiple CPUs or CPU cores without modifying the source code can simply recompile using automatic parallelization.

Virtualization encourages experimentation with compiler optimizations. Administrators can easily recompile applications with advanced optimizations and create virtual machines with the resulting binaries. They can then test the virtual machines side by side with production servers to gauge the results before moving the new binaries to production.

Conclusion

Virtualization, with its ability to run multiple operating systems on a single host, enables server consolidation and cost savings from higher hardware utilization rates. However, using less hardware to provide the same level of service can create a single point of failure, as a single hardware platform now hosts multiple logical servers. This places a greater emphasis on stable hardware platforms and server management solutions to quickly detect and deal with any problems that arise. VMM vendors offer complete management solutions that allow administrators to monitor and control virtual machines from a central management console. Vendors of traditional management consoles are also integrating support for virtual machine software. These management solutions allow the IT department to take control of the virtual infrastructure and realize the advantages of virtualization in flexibly responding to changing needs.

The next chapter takes a closer look at how virtualization can be used to further improve IT security.

Chapter 9

Security

> *Solitude is often the best society.*
>
> —Proverb

The IT department plays a key role in the productivity of a company by keeping the company's network and its data secure from intruders and attackers. Viruses, worms, Trojans, denial of service attacks, and spyware all hamper individual productivity and are a huge drain of company resources. IT professionals are responsible for many aspects of security, including establishing the corporate security policy, managing and preventing virus outbreaks, and maintaining information privacy and integrity. With many tools at their disposal, they are continually challenged to stay one step ahead of adversaries that would threaten the company's information security. Virtualization can be an additional, effective tool to help IT manage these types of security threats.

Qualities that Enhance Security

The hardware virtualization mechanisms in Intel® Virtualization Technology isolate virtual machines from one another; failures or compromises in one virtual machine do not affect the operation of the others. This quality is used as the foundation for many security-oriented scenarios. In addition, virtualization support in the processor allows virtual machine monitor (VMM) software to be smaller and less complex, which reduces the opportunity for attacks on the VMM itself.

Hardware virtualization also encourages *specialization* and *simplicity,* qualities that can also be used to enhance security. IT managers can create virtual machines with a limited set of services and operating system components. Each virtual machine can be specially "tailored," decreasing the number of unanticipated interactions among the software and limiting exposure if a partition is compromised; the fewer things running, the fewer unanticipated interactions and vulnerabilities.

Creating multiple virtual machines also allows the IT department to set policy on a per-virtual machine basis. Doing so provides a finer grain of administrative control of resources, such as network bandwidth, than if all of the services were running on a single physical server.

Finally, the ability to deliver an entire software stack, including the operating system, in a virtual machine offers a way for the IT department to ensure that client machines adhere to the corporate security policies by distributing an IT-validated image for employees to use.

These qualities—isolation, specialization, simplicity, and the portability of an entire virtual machine—are put to use in the scenarios that follow.

Containment and Quarantine

The SQL Slammer worm first appeared on January 25, 2003 and spread rapidly throughout the Internet, infecting about 75,000 victims within 10 minutes. The worm dramatically slowed down Internet traffic, causing the collapse of numerous routers under the burden of traffic generated by infected servers. The worm exploited two buffer overflow bugs in Microsoft's SQL Server and Data Engine (MSDE) products.

It is events like these that cause IT professionals to lose sleep at night. Viruses, Trojans, spyware, buffer overruns, SQL injection attacks, and the like are constant threats to corporate security. Once on the corporate network, these attacks can spread quickly, infecting machines at an exponentially increasing rate.

Viruses can attack servers by exploiting simple implementation flaws like unchecked buffers.[1] If an adversary successfully exploits this defect, it can execute code in the address space of the compromised process with the same rights and privileges as the compromised process. The

---

[1] The source code does not ensure that some input does not overrun the buffer meant to hold it. This vulnerability allows an attacker to execute arbitrary code in the context of the running application.

malicious software may gain full access to the server and could be able to modify operating system files, create user accounts, modify access control lists, and so on. More importantly, the compromised system becomes a launching pad for further attacks, both inside the firewall and outside to other companies.

The IT professional can use virtualization's ability to isolate software stacks into separate virtual machines to contain the damage wrought by a compromised platform—server, desktop, or mobile. An adversary that manages to gain access to one of the VMs does not automatically have access to the others running on the platform and intrusions can be confined to the VM in which they occur, minimizing the overall impact due to a security breach. Virtualization's hardware-based mechanisms separate the virtual machines, keeping any misbehaving partitions from directly accessing and disrupting the others, as Figure 9.1 shows.

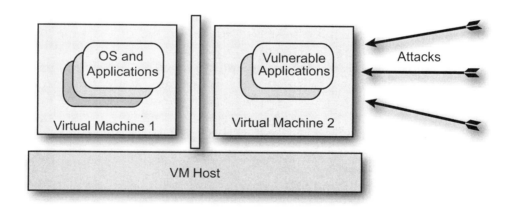

Figure 9.1   Containing the Effects of Security Breaches

Partitioning Services

For example, a company's Web server could be run in its own partition, isolated from other services running in other virtual machines on the host platform. Then, if an external adversary is able to exploit a security flaw in the Web server, the other services running in other VMs are not directly accessible to the attacker. If the network administrator has also configured the access lists for the Web server VM to not allow outgoing connections to the local network, the intruder can be contained to the compromised partition, blocking its reach into the corporate network; the intruder is effectively boxed in.

While it is possible to implement the same strategy using physical hardware, it is much more costly. The IT professional must deploy many servers with simple, specialized configurations, which will suffer from the same problems associated with underutilization—increased hardware, energy, and space costs— as the previous chapter discussed. Virtualization balances the needs to keep costs under control while providing the flexibility to implement many smaller security partitions.

Another benefit to using a virtual machine approach is that when a virtual machine is compromised, the IT professional can discard the compromised VM and revert to a previously saved snapshot, getting the service back up and running quickly.

Creating Internet Access Partitions

The Internet has become an indispensable tool for the office worker. Unfortunately, Internet access presents risks for the corporation. In particular, when using a browser to surf the Web, adversaries can disguise downloads to trick a user into downloading spyware or viruses, which can then propagate to other machines inside the corporate firewall. In addition, many applications are becoming Web applications and are subject to the same problems as Web browsing. For example, employees may log onto personal, Web-based e-mail accounts from work, inside the corporate firewall, bypassing any virus protection on the corporate mail server. Instant messaging also has its risks. Users can be tricked into clicking a link in a bogus instant message. These messages appear to be from someone the user knows, but then replicate and send themselves to other people on the user's list of contacts. Many other media allow viruses to propagate, such as executable e-mail attachments, image files with design or implementation flaws that permit code to be attached and run when the image is opened, and macros attached to office documents.

Most businesses try to intercept viruses before they infect the network. They try to block them at the gateway, or block them on the client machines by installing an antivirus application on each employee's computer. However, this approach cannot be 100-percent effective because it is reactive—viruses are first discovered in the wild, then virus software vendors analyze them, and finally these vendors distribute updates to the signature files that allow the virus scanning engine to detect the new virus. To be effective, the IT department must ensure that everyone's antivirus signature files are always up to date. Even so, there can be a significant delay from the time a new virus is released onto the Internet to when the virus signature files on client machines are actually able to detect and prevent the virus from propagating. Infections will happen, and the corporation must have a strategy for *containment* as well as prevention.

The cost to companies can be high, including decreased worker productivity due to clogged e-mail systems, reduced network bandwidth, and unavailability of services as they are cleaned up. The IT department must deal with the aftermath of an infection—searching and eradicating the virus, repairing damaged system, and so on.

As in the data center, virtualization can help contain viruses that infect worker systems. The ability to run multiple virtual machines on a single host makes it easy to have a separate partition dedicated to Internet use—an *Internet appliance*—from which the user can browse the Web, use instant messaging, and perform other Internet activities. Applications that could potentially be conduits for malware are grouped into this virtual machine. Malware that infects this partition can then be contained and prevented from spreading to other virtual machines. Another benefit of virtualization is that users can periodically dispose of and refresh this Internet access partition with a new, known-to-be-clean partition, quickly ensuring that their machines are not infected. Like disposable rubber gloves used by a nurse or doctor to limit the spread of germs and disease, refreshing this partition can help limit the spread of infection.

Creating a Network Monitor Partition

The hardware-based separation of virtual machines does not, by itself, limit the spread of viruses to other computers. While virtual machines do not have direct access to other virtual machines on the same host, they can still have network access and can reach the other virtual machines, as well as other hosts, over the network.

Using virtualization it is possible to route all network traffic to and from the VMs through a single management virtual machine to create a choke point[2] for all network traffic. Then, a dedicated *supervisor,* running on the management VM, can monitor the network activity for patterns of infection. The supervisor, when it detects patterns that suggest virus propagation, can send a notification to administrative

---

[2] A choke point forces attackers to use a single channel that you can monitor and control.

management consoles as well as cut off the virtual machine's networking capabilities, effectively quarantining the machine. Figure 9.2 shows how this network monitor partition protects the rest of the network from a "surge," such as a virus outbreak, originating from a particular computer.

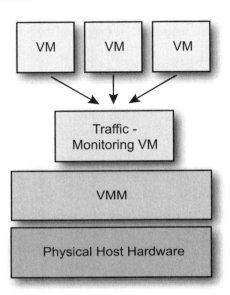

Figure 9.2   A Network Monitor Partition

For example, the SQL Slammer worm mentioned previously propagated itself to other SQL servers on the network by putting together a special 376-byte packet and sending it to randomly chosen IP addresses on port 1434. When a vulnerable machine received the packet, it also became infected and it, too, began to propagate to other network hosts. This general pattern—sending the same packet to random hosts on the network—could be detected by a supervisor running on a service partition, which would then isolate the source of these packets from the rest of the network.

The special partition that monitors network traffic could be part of a larger partition dedicated to management functionality. See the section "Creating an IT Service Partition."

Implementing a Honeypot

In his book on military strategies and tactics, Sun Tzu says to "know thy enemy and know thyself, find naught in fear for 100 battles." Learning more about your enemy's strategies and tactics can help one anticipate and prepare for different modes of attack. In the IT world, one way to learn about how an adversary gains unauthorized access to computer systems and what he or she does once he or she has access is to use a *honeypot*.

A honeypot is a computer system put in place solely to lure attackers and find out more about them. The IT professional deploying the honeypot monitors the activities of the intruder in order to learn about its methods and help steel the corporate network against future attempts at unauthorized use. If the honeypot is successful, the intruder will not know that he or she is being tricked or that his or her every move is being monitored and logged. Honeypots are designed to entice; they mimic systems that an intruder would like to break into, such as Web servers, e-mail servers, or FTP servers.

Honeypots typically have firewalls, but they work in the opposite way that a normal firewall works: instead of filtering the traffic that comes into the system from the Internet, the honeypot firewall allows all traffic in but restricts what the system can send back out. If the honeypot is not properly configured, an intruder can gain access and use it as a launching point for further attacks into real hosts on the network. Figure 9.3 illustrates how a honeypot limits the reach of intruders.

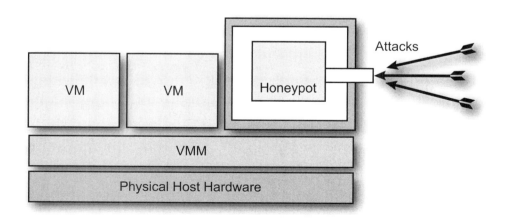

Figure 9.3   Trapped inside a Honeypot

Here are some uses for honeypots:

■ As a surveillance and early-warning tool. Because any activity occurring on the honeypot is unauthorized and can be considered malicious, you know when you're under attack.

■ To help network administrators learn how intruders probe and exploit vulnerabilities to gain access to systems. By logging all of the activity on the machine, a network administrator can study the activities of intruders to identify weaknesses and gain insight into attack methodologies. The administrator can then use this information to better protect production systems and to help make them less vulnerable to future attacks.

■ To gather forensic information to help law enforcement officials prosecute intruders.

■ To identify specific remote hosts that are performing illegal activities over legal channels, such as sending spam to an e-mail server. Since all activity on the honeypot is unauthorized, the sources of spam can be identified and blocked.

Honeypots are available in many different implementations, but there are two general categories: low-interaction and high-interaction.

■ *Low-interaction.* This type of honeypot typically emulates only certain parts of the operating system, such as the networking stack, or provides only certain services, such as an FTP server. A low-interaction honeypot is easier to deploy and maintain and has minimal risk; the emulated services can contain the attacker's activity. However, they gather limited information and are designed to capture only known attacks.

■ *High-interaction.* This type of honeypot does not emulate real systems or network services, but instead, uses the real thing. Special computers are dedicated to the task and use real applications and services. High-interaction honeypots are far more complex to deploy and have greater risk; they can be compromised completely, allowing an adversary to gain full access to the system and to use it to launch further network attacks. They are also more expensive than low-interaction honeypots given the hardware costs and additional maintenance required, especially if an organization wants to deploy many high-interaction honeypots. However, high-interaction honeypots can capture far more information that could prove to be quite valuable if it prevents future intrusions.

Using Virtualization

With virtualization, IT professionals seeking to improve network security can create high-interaction honeypots without the associated costs of a hardware-based solution. They can set up a complete software stack that contains the operating system, services, and monitoring software in a virtual machine. Many of these honeypot VMs can be deployed on a single physical server, saving on hardware resources, and are indistinguishable from real hardware-based systems. The preconfigured honeypot virtual machines can be provided with others in the organization and in the IT profession, making it easier to share and deploy best practices throughout the Internet. If attacked, the virtual machine can be easily duplicated to allow multiple people to investigate the break-in simultaneously; in effect the entire virtual machine snapshot, not just log files, becomes evidence in a security evaluation.

Testing Exploits in a Contained Environment

Sometimes, the best way to understand a threat to network security is to see it in action. Network administrators, working to counter the latest security exploit and secure the local network, may want to test a fix for the exploit without putting a production system or network at risk. They would like to experiment and test the fix prior to deploying it in the real production environment.

With virtualization, network administrators don't have to shy away from testing potentially dangerous exploits or suspicious programs in order to gauge the impact to their networks. Using a simulated network of virtual machines allows an administrator to work with the security exploit in a contained environment, with no danger to the host or network. The network of VMs can be set up to match the production environment but isolated from the production network, creating a *virtual security testing lab* where the exploit is put "under a microscope." Before introducing the exploit into the virtual environment, copies of the VMs can be made to facilitate retesting. If a potential fix fails, the administrator can simply delete the virtual machines and fall back to the previous snapshots.

Specialization and Simplicity

Hardware virtualization lowers the cost of deploying additional machines. Administrators can deploy many operating systems on a single platform and easily add more. This quality of virtualization encourages the use of specialized virtual machines. A benefit of this approach is that each virtual machine becomes simpler; and a simpler configuration can be more easily validated for security. The following usage scenarios emphasize specialization and simplicity to show how the use of virtualization can enhance security.

Building "Tailored" Servers

Security professionals consider simplicity a virtue. Keeping things simple makes them easier to understand and analyze for security vulnerabilities. Complexity, on the other hand, offers a breeding ground for defects. In software development, the complexity of a solution can hide unanticipated and undiscovered flaws. Complex programs are therefore more likely to have bugs than simpler solutions; and these bugs often lead to security weaknesses and loopholes. Following this principle challenges network security administrators to remove all unnecessary functionality from servers.

A virtual machine system has the ability to host multiple virtual machines on a single platform. If you combine this capability with the trend towards simplicity for the sake of security, the result is a system of smaller, *specialized* partitions that is easier to analyze for security vulnerabilities than a similar monolithic solution. The partitions can be purpose-specific and more focused in the functionality they provide. As such, they are less likely to be interfered with by other services or compromised by unanticipated interactions.

Here are the kinds of services you can place in dedicated virtual machines on a single virtual machine host.

- LDAP – directory services
- FTP server
- Web server
- VPN server
- SQL database
- SAP

Each of the partitions becomes a kind of "utility service" that can be analyzed for security vulnerabilities and managed independently from the others. Instead of having a union of all of the services on a single platform, they are partitioned as desired across multiple virtual machines, as Figure 9.4 shows.

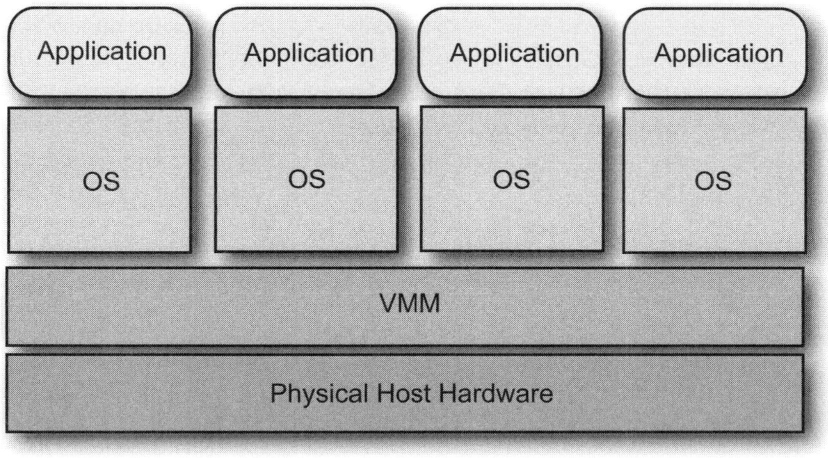

Figure 9.4   Many Simple Utility Partitions

In addition to security, a simpler arrangement offers these benefits:

■ The overall system is more robust. A service that fails in one partition will not cause the others to fail. They can be reset independently.

■ Each service can be selected and deployed without an operating system constraint; a network administrator can select the best application and operating system for the job.

■ The services can be mixed and matched on hardware platforms to achieve the highest processor and network utilization.

Creating an IT Service Partition

To decrease the total cost of ownership, OEMs have, over the years, included more and more management features on business PC platforms. Using central management consoles, network administrators can monitor and control these PCs from a distance, helping to secure the enterprise network environment by intelligently controlling its endpoints.

Software services run on the PCs and provide one end of the communication infrastructure. The software services running on a typical desktop PC operating system are only as secure as the local administrator's account. A savvy user can override settings and circumvent security policy.

With virtualization, it is possible to create a special *service partition,* a dedicated, headless[3] virtual machine that has special privileges relative to the other virtual machines. Using products such as VMWare ACE†, access to the service partition can be limited to only network administrators. The partition exists not for the user, but for the enforcement of the corporate security polity; it is an extension of IT security mechanisms to the user's PC.

The service partition should have access to the network traffic of all of the virtual machines so that it can inspect and filter incoming packets based on policy. The policy itself can be cached locally on this partition, safe from tampering. The partition becomes a place to deploy management software that is independent from the user's operating system, applications, and configuration.

Management Tools to Go

The ability to boot a PC from a CD-ROM is a convenient feature. Network administrators can have a toolkit of their favorite Linux distribution with the latest versions of popular open source network security tools—port scanning, packet sniffing, sniffer detection, vulnerability scanning, packet construction, network monitoring, intrusion detection, and so on—ready to use from any PC to diagnose and fix network and client PC problems as the need arises. Instead of disturbing a user's environment by rebooting a PC to load this management toolkit, an administrator can simply start a virtual machine, perhaps from a USB key. All of the tools will then be available to the administrator, in the administrator's preferred environment. At the same time, the user's desktop is available to help the administrator to diagnose problems.

---

[3] A "headless partition" is one that does not have a local user interface. The term comes from a PC or server without a monitor—it's "head."

Client Platform Deployment

People make mistakes. If a security system relies upon employees flawlessly executing a process, it is doomed to fail. A better strategy is to carefully do something right once and then distribute the results for others to use. For the IT professional, virtualization creates opportunities to improve the security of client computers by creating and distributing standardized virtual machines.

Deploying Standardized VPN Clients

A category of virtualization scenarios is *exclusive access and control.* Usages in this category share a common pattern. This pattern has a *user* and a *service provider.* The user must use the service provider's full platform, including hardware. The service provider needs exclusive access and full control over its platform in order to monitor it and keep the software up to date. The service provider doesn't want anyone else to modify the machine's configuration, because doing so could impair the delivery of a service. Without virtualization, the service provider must deliver a complete platform to the user, as Figure 9.5 shows.

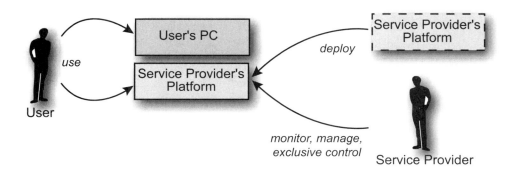

Figure 9.5   Exclusive Access and Control without Virtualization

The drawback to this situation is that the service provider must incur significant costs to provide the hardware to the user, even though there may be sufficient computational resources at the user's disposal.

This pattern can be easily updated to incorporate virtualization. As long as the platform is virtualization capable, the user can allow the service provider to run and have complete control of a virtual machine on this platform. Instead of delivering a physical machine, the service provider can simply deliver a virtual machine. The user still owns the physical machine; the service provider "owns" and controls the partition. The service provider no longer has to deploy physical hardware to the user, saving on both the hardware itself and the associated deployment costs. Figure 9.6 shows the new, simpler situation when exclusive access and control is implemented using virtualization.

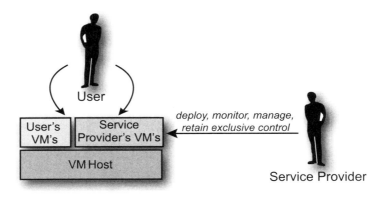

Figure 9.6   Exclusive Access and Control with Virtualization

For example, consider a company that implements a strict security policy intended to ensure the security of the corporate network. As part of this policy, the IT department requires strict control over the clients that are allowed to connect to the network using VPN software. A company employee wants to conveniently access the corporate network from a home PC. However, home PCs, which often run insecure wireless networks, are potential conduits for virus attacks on the corporate network. So the employee is not allowed to work from his or her home computer because it doesn't have the validated operating system build with approved VPN application.

Virtualization can resolve this situation. Instead of having to deploy company-supplied computers, the IT department can deploy an approved, standard IT virtual machine build instead. The employee at home can't modify the standard build and uses it exclusively to access the network; in effect, using a virtual notebook PC instead of a physical one. The result is more convenience for the employee and less expense for the company.

Deploying Patched Operating Systems

Attackers regularly discover and exploit flaws in operating systems. As these exploits become known, operating system vendors release patches. A company's IT department must validate security patches for use in the local computing environment, testing them against their standard end-user applications to make sure they still work correctly. However, IT can't test all client configurations, particularly in cases where end users customize their own environments or attempt to run unauthorized environments.

As organizations get larger, the support burden associated with operating system patches increases as more and more users encounter installation and upgrade problems, as Figure 9.7 depicts.

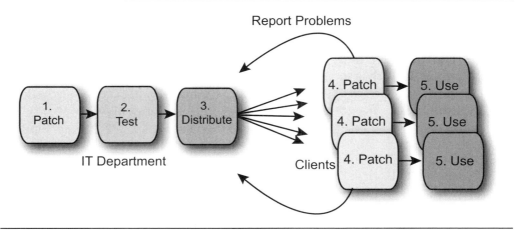

Figure 9.7   Deployment of Patches with Support Feedback Burden

Virtualization can simplify the distribution of an approved machine image to many users. Instead of distributing a patch and requiring all users to install it, a company can utilize a "copy exactly" strategy for scaling the distribution of operating system patches. The company configures and tests a single virtual machine image and then distributes that image for everyone to use. The staff is up and running quickly on the new image with no installation hassles, using a method that scales easily as the organization grows. Figure 9.8 shows the new, simpler pattern resulting from this approach.

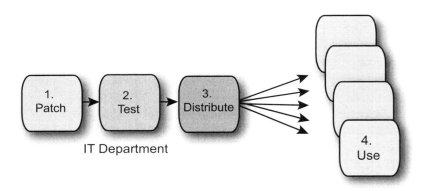

Figure 9.8   Delivering the Entire Virtual Machine

The tested virtual machine image could contain the company's standard office tools, pre-configured and ready to use. A limitation of this approach is that there are not yet tools to transfer incremental changes and settings from one VM to another. When the user installs additional software or changes the configuration of his environment, these changes would have to be brought forward to the new updated virtual machine.

Conclusion

In the endless arms race that is the life of the IT professional concerned about security, virtualization is an effective tool. Virtualization exhibits qualities that can be used to enhance the security of both servers and end-user platforms. This chapter has presented many security-related usage scenarios that take advantage of these qualities; most importantly, the ability of a VMM to isolate virtual machines from each other using hardware features supplied by Intel Virtualization Technology. There are many other security scenarios that can and will be developed using techniques similar to those presented here.

The next chapter will look at how virtualization can be used to support another facet of the IT professional's responsibilities: ensuring that services and data are available so that business can proceed uninterrupted.

Chapter **10**

Robustness and Availability

True stability results when presumed order and presumed disorder are balanced. A truly stable system expects the unexpected, is prepared to be disrupted, waits to be transformed.

—Tom Robbins

Servers that provide critical business data must be robust so that they are always available to corporate users who depend on them. IT departments go to great lengths to achieve high availability by using strategies like replication and redundancy, and they may maintain backup systems to come online immediately in case a primary system fails. IT departments proactively monitor servers for signs of hardware failures and routinely perform low-level system maintenance to keep them running smoothly. Administrators also balance the loads on servers to maintain optimal performance. Virtualization—in particular, the ability to duplicate an entire virtual machine and move it across distinct physical hosts—can simplify these high-availability scenarios.

Some server applications may occasionally stop responding or otherwise destabilize their host environments and neighboring applications. Virtualization can be used in these situations to increase robustness by isolating potentially destabilizing applications into separate virtual machines, containing their impact on other applications.

Maintaining the integrity and availability of corporate data is also an important responsibility for IT and an essential element of a business continuity plan. The IT department must be able to back up and restore data and to quickly respond to and recover from disasters to keep the business running as smoothly as possible. Administrators can use virtualization to simplify server backup and recovery, making it a key part of a disaster recovery plan.

Virtual Machine Migration

By encapsulating a guest operating system's state within a virtual machine (VM), virtualization makes it possible to decouple the guest from the host hardware on which it is currently running and to move, or *migrate,* it to a different platform. This conceptually simple, but profound, capability facilitates many of the scenarios described in this chapter.

In general, migration of an application from one physical host to another must balance *downtime,* the period during which the service is unavailable to users. It must also balance *total migration time,* the time from when the migration is started to when it is completed and the original host can safely be taken down for maintenance, upgrade, or repair.

Pre-virtualization attempts at migration involved migrating individual processes, such as a running instance of a Web server, to a different machine. This process-level approach had numerous drawbacks. For example, a process depends on many operating system-level resources, such as file descriptors, network connections, and shared memory segments, which make it very difficult to completely and correctly migrate all of the information upon which a process depends. To handle these external dependencies, some implementations of process-level migration required that the original machine remain available to the migrated process to remotely service system calls from the newly migrated process. This architecture, shown in Figure 10.1, requires the original machine to service calls from the migrated process and prevents administrators from taking down the original machine for servicing. It also negatively impacts the performance of the migrated process because calls are routed over the network instead of handled locally.

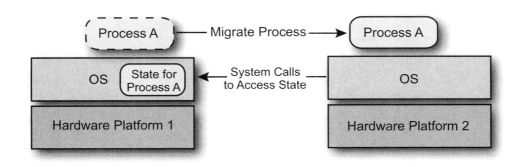

Figure 10.1   Process Level Migration

Using virtualization, an administrator can migrate an entire virtual machine image, including all operating system and application state, from one host to another. Migrating an entire operating system and all of its applications as a unit avoids many of the limitations inherent in process-level migration and offers two key benefits: First, the application-level state and the state maintained by the operating system on behalf of applications, like network connections, are migrated along with the applications themselves. The entire machine image snapshot at a point in time is transferred to the new host. For client/server applications like streaming media servers, this means that users don't have to reconnect to the server. Second, once the virtual machine has been migrated to the new host, the original host machine does not have to remain available and network accessible to service system calls on behalf of the migrated process. The original machine can be taken out of service for maintenance or repair. Figure 10.2 illustrates the virtual machine migration.

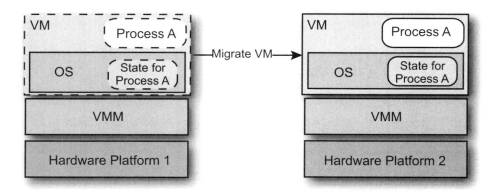

Figure 10.2 Virtual Machine Migration

Not only can entire virtual machines be moved to another host, products such as VMware's VMotion[†] facilitate *live virtual machine migration.* An administrator can use VMotion to dynamically move a virtual machine, on the fly, to another hardware platform. Some degradation in performance will occur during any live migration scheme (for example, sending VM images between two hosts consumes network bandwidth that would otherwise be available to applications), but by carrying out the majority of migration while the virtual machine continues to run, administrators can use live VM migration to decrease service downtimes and lessen the impact on users.

Migrating services at the virtual machine level has an additional benefit: it enables a clear separation of concerns between the operator of a data center or cluster and the users and administrators of the virtual machines themselves. Administrators don't need to give the operator the root logon to access the operating system as part of the migration process. The operator simply migrates the entire virtual machine, without the need for internal access.

Robustness and Reliability

With virtual machine migration, server administrators can more easily handle hardware failures, balance the workload among machines, and perform hardware maintenance operations, as these scenarios demonstrate.

Managing Hardware Failures

Although servers can often achieve impressive uptime rates, no machine can run forever. Every machine experiences occasional hardware failures. In these cases, administrators, with a high degree of fault tolerance in mind, need to quickly move the workload to alternate servers to get the services hosted on the affected machine running again and to minimize the service outage for users.

Failure prediction agents run on servers and alert administrative management consoles of intermittent and impending failures. Anticipating a hardware failure, an administrator might use a strategy that involves mirrored or replicated servers. The administrator maintains a parallel server on standby, ready to take over if the primary server fails. However, maintaining this duplicate hardware is expensive.

Instead, administrators can use virtualization techniques to achieve fault tolerance and to more readily recover from system failures. They can use a virtual machine to mirror a physical server. For example, an administrator can use VMware's P2V Assistant to take a snapshot of a physical machine, reducing it to a virtual machine that is transported to a different physical host. Administrators can also copy a virtual machine and send it to a separate machine. In either case, the backup virtual machine can be activated if a failure occurs on the primary physical host machine. These virtual machines mirror the primary server and act as failover servers to ensure high availability. Using a virtual machine for this capability delivers improved quality of service at a lower operational cost.

Failover Automation

In addition to a manual response, administrators can develop scripts to automate failover. The VMware Virtual Infrastructure SDK, for example, allows administrators to write scripts to access servers and manipulate the VMs hosted under VMware ESX Server[†] when these hosts are managed by VMware VirtualCenter management software. Using this SDK, administrators can script virtually all of the functionality that is available interactively from the management console, creating a powerful fault-tolerance capability.

For example, consider a server with a failing network adapter. Failure prediction agents running on the server detect the failing adapter and send alerts to the VMWare VirtualCenter management console to inform administrators of the intermittent failures. A script running in

VirtualCenter then calls the VMotion functions to move the virtual machines hosted on the failing server to another server on the network. Figure 10.3 illustrates this script-driven approach to failover.

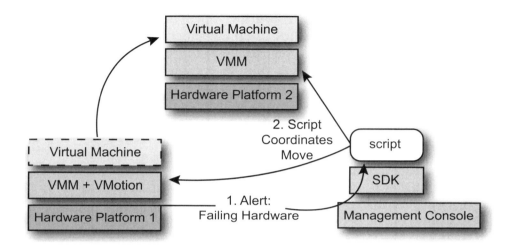

Figure 10.3   Events Trigger Scripts That Use SDK to Move VMs

Once the virtual machines have been safely migrated to another host, the failing server can be taken down, serviced, and brought back online. The administrator can then migrate the virtual machines back to the original host, again with little effect on end user applications. Using the transportability of virtual machines, administrators can keep critical services up and running for end users with minimal interruption.

Updating and Servicing Hardware

Users of networked computer systems occasionally encounter notices that let them know about an upcoming planned outage in service:

Scheduled Maintenance

This server will be unavailable starting from noon tomorrow for maintenance. Please make sure you are logged off during that time. Estimated downtime is 3-4 hours.

Our apologies for any inconvenience.

Administrators often need to make software or hardware changes, upgrades or repairs to keep systems running smoothly. They schedule the maintenance operations to provide sufficient notice to users and to make sure users are logged off the system at that time so that they can remove it from service and perform the scheduled maintenance. Maintenance tasks include replacing an aging disk drive, adding memory, upgrading a processor, upgrading a software version, and so on. It is not uncommon for the machine to be out of service for many hours as maintenance is performed.

In addition to handling unplanned failures, administrators can use virtualization to provide users with higher availability during planned service and maintenance operations. Using a technology like VMware's VMotion, an administrator can migrate entire virtual machines to alternate hosts, immediately freeing the original machine for maintenance, but without disrupting user sessions. The administrator can then upgrade memory, for example, and have the machine up and running again in minutes, ready to transfer back the workload. Users are unaware of the maintenance operation and service is not interrupted.

Virtualization provides an additional benefit for companies that haven't standardized on equipment across the data center: Identical platforms are not necessary to migrate the host machines. The virtual machines will run on any platform that is capable of hosting the virtual machine monitor (VMM), including older equipment. Being able to use more machines to host virtual machines provides an addition degree of flexibility and expands an administrator's options.

Balancing Workloads

In addition to moving workloads between machines to facilitate a planned maintenance operation, administrators can also move workloads to balance utilization across many servers in a cluster. Administrators can dynamically respond to temporary spikes in server workloads by moving

VMs to distribute the load across multiple systems. As with the other scenarios, administrators can use SDKs and scripting to automate this capability.

The combination of virtualization and VM migration gives administrators a fine degree of control over server resources. First, administrators can use virtualization to increase resource utilization, consolidating hardware and distributing the workload across machines. Next, administrators can monitor the servers and dynamically redistribute workloads, optimizing system utilization in real time based on changing workload demand. This combination of static workload distribution and dynamically adapting to changing conditions maximizes utilization and the return on hardware investment; less hardware is required, servers are kept busy, and no particular server is overloaded. This type of flexibility can transform data centers and clusters into very dynamic, responsive environments that run smoothly and provide the best performance to users.

Increasing Reliability through Fault Isolation

Companies can attempt to consolidate onto fewer servers without using virtualization. Server applications such as domain controllers, DNS, DHCP, Web servers, and database servers can be squeezed into fewer hardware platforms. However, most application failures are caused by software faults. Consolidating services without virtualization can result in a less robust system, because a failure in a single application can bring down other applications running on the same server. Virtualization provides a logical isolation between virtual machines. Fault isolation contains the disruption caused by software faults to a single virtual machine; if a Web server in one partition experiences a fault, for example, it will not bring down the DNS server in another partition. To further increase availability, scripts can detect a program failure and automatically restart, in seconds, the failing VM. The result is increased robustness and higher availability of services.

This logical isolation between virtual machines also encourages the use of single focus VMs. Any software required for a single logical service is brought together onto a single virtual machine. These VMs are like "server appliances" that provide a single service to the network and are not able to disturb each other. Administrative policy, such as bandwidth limitations, can be applied to the machine as well, giving administrators well-partitioned control over the services they offer.

Business Continuity and Data Availability

While the Year 2000 bug turned out to be a smaller problem than anticipated, recent world events demonstrate that companies must be prepared; they need a response plan in place that can manage a terrorist incident, natural disaster, or other disruption and outline steps to quickly resume any critical functions that have been interrupted. An effective business continuity plan considers how the essential functions of the business would survive a loss of buildings, staff, IT systems, records, or other information, so that the business can continue to operate and provide its services to employees and customers. The plan assesses the risks an organization faces and the potential impact that these risks would have on the organization and its operating environment. Risks for the company to consider include:

- Natural disasters such as fire, flood, or severe weather.

- IT or infrastructure failure, such as electrical power failure, equipment failures, or other hardware failure.

- Organized and deliberate disruption, such as vandalism or terrorism (an organization might be affected by a terrorist attack even if it is not the specific target of the attack).

- Industrial unrest or other civil disorder.

The business continuity plan determines the critical business functions that must survive any disruptive event and provides the timeline for their recovery; in particular, the availability of services and of data.

Businesses typically use redundancy as the primary strategy to implement a continuity plan. For example, performing regular data backups minimizes the loss of company data, and maintaining duplicate servers in alternate locations helps to ensure that the company can respond to a disaster and continues to provide services even if company data is lost or the primary location is unavailable. Both backup and disaster recovery are essential elements of an effective business continuity strategy. Virtualization can play an important role in backup and disaster recovery, and the efficiencies gained from using virtualization can help companies save money and improve their recovery time.

Implementing Data Backups

A company's most valuable asset, after its people, is data. Accordingly, companies make safe copies of data to ensure that its information is protected from events like data corruption, hardware failure, or fire, and continues to be available to the people who need it. An effective backup system is nonintrusive and reliable, and it can copy data with little effect on production systems. Backup systems should be tested regularly to make sure they maintain their effectiveness. Just as important as a reliable backup is the ability to recover the same data in a timely fashion to prevent any interruptions to business. The data may be safe, but if it can't be quickly restored, the business will suffer.

You can approach the implementation of backup using virtualization in one of two ways: The first strategy you can use is a standard backup solution. With this approach the virtual machine appears to the backup solution as a physical machine and is backed up and restored in the same way. The effect on the organization is minimal because the backup process uses existing systems. Other than the seamless integration of virtual machines into an existing backup infrastructure, you derive no direct benefit from using virtualization. A second, more interesting, alternative is to treat virtual machines as files and to back up all of the files that comprise a virtual machine. This approach saves not only the data hosted by the virtual machines, but everything else as well: all of the programs, user accounts, configuration information, and so on. It is a snapshot of the virtual machine at a moment in time. Figure 10.4 shows a list of the files associated with three snapshots of a Windows Server 2003 virtual machine created by VMware Workstation.

```
        8,664  Windows Server 2003 Enterprise Edition.nvram
2,171,600,896  Windows Server 2003 Enterprise Edition.vmdk
  536,870,912  Windows Server 2003 Enterprise Edition.vmem
        1,615  Windows Server 2003 Enterprise Edition.vmsd
   18,684,604  Windows Server 2003 Enterprise Edition.vmss
        1,108  Windows Server 2003 Enterprise Edition.vmx
6,174,539,776  Windows Server 2003 Enterprise Edition-000001.vmdk
2,044,002,304  Windows Server 2003 Enterprise Edition-000002.vmdk
   82,378,752  Windows Server 2003 Enterprise Edition-000003.vmdk
       18,011  Windows Server 2003 Enterprise Edition-Snapshot1.vmsn
       18,018  Windows Server 2003 Enterprise Edition-Snapshot2.vmsn
       18,018  Windows Server 2003 Enterprise Edition-Snapshot3.vmsn
```

Figure 10.4   Files Used by VMware Snapshots

Backing up an entire virtual machine is a simple solution. The data need not be extracted from the host platform; instead of using backup tools to "reach in" to the virtual machine to back up only the data, an administrator can take a snapshot of a virtual machine and then back up the associated files, saving the entire virtual machine state. If data is corrupted, the administrator can restore the most recent snapshot and restart that VM.

As previously mentioned, administrators can use the VMware Virtual Infrastructure SDK to write scripts that access servers and manipulate the virtual machines they are hosting, automate server backups, or save a snapshot of a virtual machine and then copy it to a safe location. Because virtual machines are simply files on a disk, it is easy to implement a VM-based backup capability.

While backup mechanisms can help keep corporate data safe and available if hardware fails, companies also need more comprehensive plans for how to respond to calamities such as a fire or natural disaster.

Implementing Disaster Recovery

Recent events have caused business to seriously consider what they would do if a serious event causes an interruption to key business functions. While it may have been possible to ignore disaster recovery before, companies now realize the importance of preparation. Disaster recovery is critical in all environments where essential corporate information is managed and stored.

Companies have disaster recovery plans to help them respond quickly to emergency situations and restore service as quickly as possible. The most common disaster recovery strategy is to maintain an alternate disaster recovery facility that duplicates the production environment; one backup server for each production server. The backup facility has critical applications on standby, ready to be activated, as needed. If a failure occurs, there is typically a delay as administrators respond to the situation and bring the backup facility online.

Most companies initially look to virtualization to increase server utilization rates and reduce hardware costs. Because of the costs of maintaining a backup facility, disaster recovery is another significant expense companies incur. Companies that use virtualization to increase server utilization can also take advantage of virtualization to implement a less expensive disaster recovery solution, eliminating the expense of a dedicated facility.

Companies with a virtual infrastructure in disparate data centers already have key elements of a disaster recovery solution in place: a remote location to serve as a backup to a primary location and a network connection between the sites. From routine maintenance to a serious outage due to a natural disaster, each site can serve as the backup for the other if a failure occurs.

The administrator can regularly create snapshots of the servers and exchange them with the alternate site. Then, if a failure occurs, the backup image of the virtual machine can be immediately deployed to any host at the other facility, minimizing downtime experienced by users.

Using virtualization to implement disaster recovery reduces the time, from days to hours, to restore services. Companies can save money because they can reliably migrate virtual machines between existing sites thereby using less hardware for a disaster recovery solution.

However, using virtualization to transform remote data centers into disaster-recovery backups for one another has challenges:

■ *More to lose.* Because each physical host is running multiple virtual machines, it becomes a single point of failure for multiple virtual machines. If one physical server goes down, so do multiple logical servers running in virtual machines. This aspect of virtualization emphasizes the need for effective management tools and hardware monitoring.

■ *Keeping track of what's running on each server.* Servers are not single function devices, but are hosting multiple virtual machines. To rebuild infrastructure after an outage, administrators will need to know exactly what virtual machines and applications were running on each physical server and which processes should be restored first.

Conclusion

IT departments can utilize virtualization to enhance availability and improve robustness and reliability in data center and cluster environments. Migration of virtual machines is the key feature that makes this possible. An administrator can migrate virtual machines to service hardware, to respond to an impending hardware failure, or to balance workloads among machines. These actions can be initiated manually from a management console and can also be automated using scripts.

Companies that previously had not seriously considered disaster recovery options are now investigating the possibilities. Fortunately, once a company has created a virtual infrastructure and has enjoyed the benefits of server consolidation and higher utilization, it can use the virtual infrastructure as part of its backup and business continuity plans. Using virtualization to implement in-house disaster recovery can save companies money when compared to the cost of maintaining a separate backup facility.

Chapter 11

Distribution and Deployment

> *Now and then I had moments of greatness, but I never knew how to duplicate it consistently.*
>
> —Ian Williams

Usage scenarios often arise where several users need exactly the same configuration on their computers. For example, companies might standardize all client machines on the same operating system and applications, set up a software development team with the same operating system and development tools, or require a testing group to use standard images to perform their regression tests. The most common approach to standardizing platforms is to describe the configuration in detail and have others carefully reproduce it on their machines.

Virtual machines (VMs) are very effective in situations like these where a single configuration must be communicated to many users. You can exercise a high degree of control over the contents of a VM—its operating system, applications, and user configuration—and distribute the result to everyone. Using VMs eliminates the effort required to describe how to duplicate a particular configuration and how to actually perform the duplication steps. Instead of communicating how to put an operating system and applications together, a single knowledgeable person can simply do it once and share the result with others. VMs are especially useful in situations where the process of duplicating the configuration is quite complicated, time consuming, or prone to error.

Virtualization also encourages users to experiment with new software. Previously, the effort required to configure a machine and the reluctance to taint a personal system, often prevented users from evaluating new software. Virtualization removes these barriers and allows users to easily experiment and evaluate without worrying about installation and configuration hassles or disturbing a production environment.

Educators and trainers need precise control over the environment their students use. The ability to create and distribute VMs allows them to establish preconfigured environments for user education and training that have identically-configured software and lessons, which minimizes configuration issues and enhances students' productivity.

This chapter presents a few of the distribution and deployment scenarios that virtualization makes possible.

Deployment and Distribution Strategies

A VM can be configured once and used many times, saving many users the time that otherwise would be required to install the operating system or applications. This approach scales well as more users require the same configuration, especially for complicated, multi-part, multi-tier installations that require a high degree of expertise to get right. Here are some deployment and distribution strategies that take advantage of this VM characteristic.

Deploying Virtual Notebook Computers

Companies with a large workforce typically configure standard notebook computers for employees. IT-approved applications, such as an office application suite and remote access software, are installed on these computers so that employees can connect to the corporate network while on the road. Over time, the computers accumulate more user-owned data and applications, potentially compromising the original IT-established secure configuration. Companies go through hardware upgrade cycles every few years as well. The company purchases new machines for employees and upgrades the old ones, requiring the users to migrate their customized environments and data to the new machines.

Companies can use virtualization to address both of these issues with notebook computer deployments. The IT department can enforce policies covering notebook use for company purposes by configuring and tightly controlling a "software appliance"—a complete end-user environment in a VM that is deployed to everyone and replaces the preconfigured laptop (see *Delivering Software Appliances* in this chapter). The user can access the corporate network from the IT VM and use company-approved applications. The user can run this VM side by side with one or more personal VMs. IT has lockdown control of its VM and the user has flexibility to use various operating systems and applications in the user-controlled partitions. Using VMs this way also simplifies the process of upgrading the user to a new machine. The user can simply migrate all VMs to the new platform and continue using them there. If the user exclusively uses VMs, the old machine is not tainted with the user's configuration and can easily be used by someone else in the organization.

By focusing on the delivery of a corporate software appliance instead of a physical notebook computer, IT departments can consider eliminating the corporate purchase of notebook computers and use employee-owned notebooks instead. The employee-owned computers do not have to be identical; they must simply be capable of hosting VMs. Early adopters, especially smaller businesses, are already attempting to make this approach work. This trend may eventually result in knowledge workers bringing their own computers to work just as many mechanics and carpenters bring their tools to work today.

However, virtual notebooks present some security implications. A physical machine provides some degree of physical security—only one person can be in possession of the machine at a time, and it is obvious if the machine has been stolen. A VM, however, can be duplicated without the knowledge of the legitimate owner. An adversary simply has to have temporary access to the machine and enough time to duplicate the VM. Even a legitimate user may copy the VM to multiple locations, such as home computers and laptops, to be able to connect to work from different locations. Companies will have to deal with this proliferation of virtual notebook machines. Clearly, companies will no longer be able to rely on perimeter security, where the "good" guys are inside and the "bad" guys are outside. Contractors, customers, and mobile workers will have free access to the corporate network from many places and from many different machines. This will place a greater emphasis on multi-factor authentication, such as biometrics, to balance the lack of possession of the physical machine.

Using Mobile Virtual Machines

People are integrating computers more and more into their everyday lives, and they would like unlimited access to their data and applications.

They can carry along a notebook computer, or just bring the data on a convenient storage device like a USB key, hoping to use the data from a different computer. However, there is no guarantee that other computers will have the required applications or the correct versions. People would really rather use their own personalized, preconfigured environment.

As software, VMs have an inherent portability that far exceeds their hardware counterparts. People can bring along their VMs—complete with their applications, data, and configuration—and then use the local computing resources available to run them (as long as the virtual machine monitor software is available).

This usage is even more important in situations where the local computing environment doesn't permit the use of an outside computer. For example, the computing environment may be administratively limited to a set of tightly controlled, pre-configured machines. In this case, the user can run the VM on the tightly controlled platform while still work in a familiar, productive environment. Figure 3.1 depicts the situation where an administrator controls a locked down environment, but the user can introduce a personal VM into this environment and execute it on the controlled host.

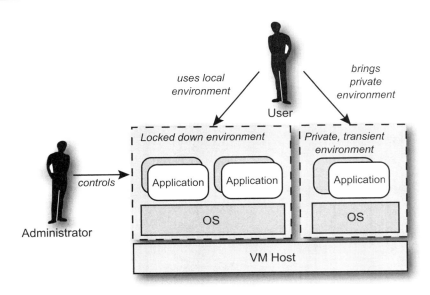

Figure 11.1   Temporary Use of a VM Host

For example, a school's computer lab may be tightly controlled by an administrator and have a limited set of applications available for student use. If the computers are capable of hosting VMs, the student can bring in a personal VM complete with a chosen operating system and applications. The student can work on the projects at school and bring the exact machine state home to continue work, without having to worry about duplicating the same environment at school. The student can use the same VM at both locations. The mobility of VMs simplifies the task of working on the same project from multiple places.

Utilizing Dual-Core Processors for Embedded Applications

At the spring 2005 Intel Developer Forum, Intel announced the launch of the dual-core Pentium® D processor and has recently announced the Intel® Core™ Duo processor, the latest processor in the Intel Centrino® mobile technology line. These processors are two examples of the many multi-core processors that Intel has planned for the desktop, laptop, and server market segments.

Dual-core processors provide two execution cores in a single processor package and significantly increase processing power without a corresponding increase in power consumption. Many processors, like the Intel Core Duo, also have intelligent power-management features to deliver significantly greater performance per watt over previous single-core processors. Multi-core processors are optimized for multithreaded applications and multitasking and remain software compatible with previous generations of the 32-bit Intel architecture processor family. A novel approach to embedded systems development combines a dual-core processor and virtualization, using one of the cores to run a real-time operating system and the other to run a general purpose operating system like Microsoft Windows.

Many embedded applications need real-time guarantees from the operating system. For example, automated manufacturing systems often require closed-loop control, where feedback is used to make changes to further control signals. The timing of events managed by the operating system must be reliable and predictable, and it must follow a deterministic schedule and predictably meet deadlines. The developer requires precise control over the relative priorities of all operations and events. However, general purpose operating systems like Windows have a multitasking kernel that fairly distributes system resources to applications, making them appropriate for desktop, server, and other general-purpose computing applications. Unfortunately, with no real-time guarantees to offer, they are inappropriate for real-time applications.

At the same time, Windows has a large software ecosystem with many excellent software development tools; and developers implementing new applications can draw from a large body of code. Embedded system designers would like to be able to take advantage of Windows software development tools and existing Windows-based applications, bringing them into real-time systems with little incremental development effort.

When working with Windows code and development tools, embedded developers can use a two-processor approach to embedded system design. The first processor, which runs Windows, is used for the non-real-time portion of the application and the second, running a real-time operating system (RTOS), implements the real-time portion of the application. Both processors can reside on a single physical motherboard, or there can be two boards in the system. In either case, the RTOS runs with a high degree of precision and can support the deterministic algorithms that embedded applications require. Because the operating systems are separate, they do not contend for CPU resources.

Unfortunately, the use of two hardware platforms has a number of drawbacks: two platforms consume more power and more space; require more resources such as power, storage, and interconnect hardware; require more programming effort; and can be more difficult to integrate.

The Virtualization Solution

It is possible to use a general purpose operating system and development tools without incurring the additional costs associated with a separate platform dedicated to achieving real-time performance. Using virtualization, a single platform based on an Intel dual-core processor can act as two separate logical platforms: one CPU for Windows and the other for the RTOS. This approach lowers the overall system costs by eliminating the need for a second processor and related hardware components. The dual-core solution provides the benefits of the multi-platform system with the design efficiencies of a single-platform system. With only one platform for which to develop software, the dual-core approach shortens the development time required for embedded solutions.

One real-time operating system that uses this approach is the TenAsys INtime[†] RTOS, which is optimized for Windows and Intel architecture. It uses VM technology to host both Windows and a protected-mode RTOS environment on an Intel Core Duo processor hardware platform. With this platform, developers can use a single development environment—Microsoft Visual Studio[†]—to target both environments.

Virtualization and multi-core processors work well together and provide interesting possibilities for cooperating virtual platforms, running potentially many different operating systems, on a single hardware platform.

Experimentation and Evaluation

Pre-built VMs make it easy to try new software and experiment with operating systems and applications that otherwise would be too difficult or time consuming to install and configure. The following scenarios review a few of the many benefits of this approach.

Releasing Internal Builds

Software development teams periodically release their build efforts to potential users and testers. These pre-release builds are delivered to meet internal milestones for testing and external milestones, such as alpha and beta, where external customers preview and provide feedback on the build. These builds usually come with installation instructions and a list of known outstanding problems. Some large applications may have complex dependencies which require other software to be installed first before the actual build can be installed and tested. If the user doesn't install the software in the right order or misses a step, the program may be unusable or, worse, leave the system in an inconsistent state. Software pre-release builds are intended to be short-lived. Users and testers exercise the software, provide feedback and report bugs, and then eventually discard it. Often, an early software release may not have an installation program, or if it does, it may not yet uninstall properly, leaving files and configuration settings on the target system.

VMs can effectively address these issues. Releasing software builds on prepared VMs allows a development team to precisely control the software configuration. Any dependencies are installed correctly because the development team understands them in detail and can carefully prepare a single golden image for others to use. When users receive the virtual machine, they can use the software immediately without the hassles of installation or configuration. Installing and configuring the software once and communicating the result increases the time that users actually have to test the software and to provide quality feedback. External users are also more likely to use the software if they know that a VM containing early software will not damage or otherwise taint their production systems.

Creating a Bundle of Tools for Evaluation

Developers who want to investigate new software development packages are often reluctant to install them on their precisely tailored development machines. Will they uninstall cleanly? Will the installation interfere with other programs or break something? Installing software can also be time consuming, taking developers away from more productive tasks. Software that might benefit the developer goes unevaluated.

Multiple software packages that could work well together exacerbate the problem. With multiple packages to install and potential interactions to consider, developers are even less likely to make the significant time investment, even if they have a spare machine and don't need to risk tainting their development system. This resistance could be called a "developer resistance threshold," and it must be overcome to get developers to install and try new software.

For example, Intel offers many software development tools that could greatly benefit developers, especially those working on high performance applications. However, Intel would like to build further awareness of the tools and explain their value to developers. In particular, the Intel C/C++ compiler is a highly optimizing compiler that has a high degree of source and binary compatibility with Microsoft Visual Studio. It is very easy to achieve significant performance gains by dropping in the Intel compiler and using its optimizations. Tools like the Intel C/C++ compiler, the VTune™ Performance Analyzer, Intel Threading Tools, and the Intel Integrated Performance Primitives can all help developers to achieve higher performing applications, especially as the industry moves to symmetric multithreading and multi-core processors. These tools can help developers make significant improvements to the run-time performance of their applications.

Unfortunately, the resistance threshold of developers is pretty high. Consider developers who do decide to evaluate these software packages. They must download and install the four distributions, acquire multiple evaluation license keys, taint their development machines with the software or prepare a separate machine for the evaluation, and spend time installing the software—all before actually getting to the evaluation itself. Given this scenario, developers are unlikely to experience the benefits these tools provide, especially the synergy that occurs when the tools are used together.

Virtualization lowers the resistance threshold of developers. One could prepare an operating system image, with the development tools and related documentation, pre-installed and ready to use for the developer. Developers can simply download these machine images or order them on a DVD, then run them in a VM. Their development machines are safe from disruption, and little time is spent on installation. They can try the tools immediately and are more likely to have a positive experience.

Delivering Software Appliances

Virtualization, combined with free and open source software, enables a new software delivery method call the *software appliance*. A software appliance is an operating system and set of applications tailored for a specific purpose, preconfigured in a VM, which users can readily download and run. Software appliances simplify software packaging, distribution, and deployment. Instead of focusing on communicating the minute details to others so that they can duplicate a configuration, a single knowledgeable person can create a VM with free and open source software and freely distribute it. Customers can quickly use software without the hassle of software installation and the frustration of compatibility issues. Software appliances allow users to focus directly on their work rather than wasting time reproducing a specific environment.

Many options are available for running software appliances, including offerings from the Xen project, Microsoft and VMware. For example, VMware offers a free VMware Player application for Windows that allows users to run VM on a Windows platform. VMware has also recently announced plans to make their GSX Server product available at no charge.

One of the most popular software appliances is the Web Browser Appliance—a free VM for download that runs the Linux operating system and the Firefox[†] Web browser. With the Web Browser Appliance, users can safely browse the Internet from within a VM. The separation of VMs into their own isolated, contained partitions prevents viruses or spyware that have been downloaded in the browser from propagating to other partitions. If the user's machine is infected with a virus or spyware, the user can delete the tainted VM and download a new one; the user's primary operating system image is unaffected. In addition to containing the spread of malware, the browser appliance can be used to safeguard personal information. Users can configure the appliance to automatically reset itself after each use so that the browser does not store personal information permanently.

Given the large amount of free and open source software available, and the clear benefits of software appliances, many more of them will probably be produced in the future. In fact, VMware is encouraging independent development by hosting a Web site dedicated to community-built VMs. People can build a VM and share it with others in the community. The VMware site has standard operating system distributions as well as highly tailored software appliances for specific target users. As virtualization becomes mainstream and people become aware of the value of software appliances, other Web sites can be expected to offer the same service.

Learning about Device Driver Development

Kernel mode programming and, in particular, device driver development is a difficult task. Developing device drivers requires an in-depth understanding of an operating system's device driver model and a detailed understanding of the target hardware. In the past, device driver developers have been experienced experts that worked exclusively for hardware companies. However, because of today's need to support many different kinds of devices in open source operating systems, more people are writing device drivers than ever before and more people are learning about driver development.

When developing drivers, kernel mode crashes are common. These types of crashes can have a serious impact on the system, such as corrupting key system files, or causing the system to lock up cold or restart. They also interfere with development because the developer has to wait for a restart or, worse, has to repair a damaged operating system. In contrast, user-level software can be developed without these concerns; the operating system's process-level protection mechanisms keep each process for disturbing others.

Developers can use a couple of approaches when writing drivers. The first is to debug the driver directly on the target machine. Kernel mode debuggers like SoftICE[†] allow developers to build and debug device drivers on a single system. Although SoftICE is a very sophisticated program, the driver can still crash the operating system, potentially corrupting system files and causing the operating system to reboot. To avoid damaging the primary software development system, many people build the driver on one machine and install the driver on a separate, sacrificial machine. The debugger runs remotely on the development system and connects to the target platform over a null-model serial cable. The target system is still subject to problems from faulty device drivers, but in this configuration the development system is unaffected.

Fortunately, virtualization makes it easier for developers to experiment with device drivers and to learn more about the basics of kernel mode programming. A device driver developer can create a snapshot of the target operating system before the device driver is installed, creating a known good configuration on which to fall back. Then, the developer can set up a remote debugger from the primary development system to the target operating system running inside the VM. Debugging occurs like a normal remote debugging session, except that both operating systems are running on the same platform. Then, when the driver crashes the operating system, it affects only the VM. The developer can simply restore the snapshot of the VM to return to a known good state. Using VMs save developers the time to restart or repair a damaged system.

This VM solution for driver development is cheaper than buying a separate target machine for debugging, saves space required for the second machine, and is much more flexible. For example, developers can have snapshots available of multiple operating systems and versions to test their new drivers. Virtualization simplifies driver development and makes kernel mode programming accessible to more developers. Any mistakes made while learning to write drivers are not serious and can be recovered from easily.

Conclusion

The "create once, share often" model made possible by virtualization is a perfect match for many distribution and deployment scenarios, such as creating standardized VMs for employees, creating software appliances to share with others, using VMs as part of a release build process, and bundling software tools for evaluation. The portability of VMs makes them convenient for using the same customized environment on many different computers. Intel's new dual core processors provide more processing power for virtualization and enable new scenarios such as dedicating a processor core to run an embedded operating system in a VM, which avoids the cost of a separate embedded processor. Finally, the isolation of VMs makes them good environments for safely learning about device drivers and kernel mode programming.

Chapter 12

The Future of Virtualization

Prediction is very difficult, especially of the future.

—Niels Bohr

Intel® Virtualization Technology, together with virtual machine monitor (VMM) software from companies such as Microsoft, VMware, XenSource, and others are bringing virtualization into the mainstream. In the coming years users will become so accustomed to the benefits of virtualization that we might wonder how anyone ever got along without it. The scenarios presented so far in this book are just the beginning; they only describe a few of the many useful applications of virtualization. Many more uses for virtualization will be invented and discovered and will continue to increase worker productivity and lower operational costs for years to come. Now that we've spent many chapters surveying the uses for virtualization that can be implemented today, this chapter gets to the fun part: speculating about future virtualization scenarios as well as how virtualization technology is likely to evolve over time.

In particular, besides the enterprise scenarios that have been covered already, there are two emerging usage model categories that might benefit from virtualization: the digital home and health care. This chapter will describe a few scenarios in these categories. Like the scenarios already presented, these scenarios rely on the qualities of virtualization, such as the isolation provided by virtual machines or the mobility of virtual machines. The chapter will continue by attempting to understand where virtualization is going by considering a few major trends in virtualization and their implications for usage models.

Digital Home Scenarios

Virtualization has many clear applications in the enterprise, but usages in the home are not as obvious. The home has different dynamics, different problems, and different usage scenarios. Still, there are a number of possible applications of virtualization in the home. For example, as home computers become a more critical part of home infrastructure—always on and providing services to other devices in the home—and as they become more powerful, with dual and quad core processors and beyond, it will be possible to run many virtual machines as background tasks on a PC. These behind-the-scenes VMs can serve a number of functions, such as replacing physical devices provided by external service providers, replacing physical devices in the home entertainment center, hosting home automation monitoring and control functions, or serving as an important part of a larger health care system that extends into the home.

Service Provider Partition

Service providers, such as cable or satellite television companies, provide set-top boxes—specialized devices that connect to the television and an input signal source and decode the incoming signal for display—to customers for use in their homes. Each set-top box is preconfigured with the software stack required to deliver the service. These devices are often just specialized computers that must be sufficiently powerful to handle features such as the ability to pause and record live television, play interactive games, or to play video-on-demand.

To connect the service, the service provider sends a technician to install the set-top box at the customer's home. This "truck roll" is a necessary expense to get the set-top box properly installed and configured. The service provider also incurs the cost of the hardware itself, covering the loss, over time, from the service subscription fees.

The service provider needs exclusive access to, and full control over, its set-top box platform in order to monitor it and keep the software up to date. The set-top boxes are not usually open platforms where third parties can install additional software; the service provider doesn't want anyone else modifying the machine's configuration, because doing so could impair the delivery of the service. The devices also must periodically connect back to the home office to look for software updates and to upload information related to billing for services. Figure 12.1 depicts the relationships between the customer, the service provider, and the equipment in the home.

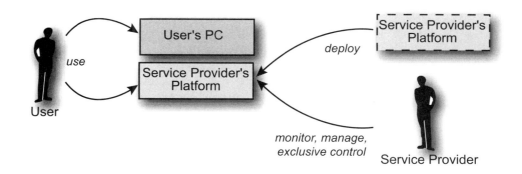

Figure 12.1   A Service Provider's Platform in the Home

The customer uses the service provider's set-top box platform, but has no control over its configuration. The service provider deploys the platform and then continues to "own it" by monitoring and managing it. If a hardware update is required to provide a new service, the service provider must deliver and install the hardware again. Meanwhile, the user often has a PC in the home—a general purpose, open platform that is networked and capable of hosting the same kind of applications that run on set-top boxes.

This situation has a number of inefficiencies that can be addressed by virtualization. In particular,

■ *The cost of installation/truck roll*—the service provider must send a technician to the customer's home to install the platform.

■ *The cost of the set-top box*—the service provider must deliver a physical platform to the user to ensure that they have complete control over the platform

■ *The cost of hardware upgrades*—if the user required new hardware in order to have a platform sufficiently powerful to receive a new service, the service provider would have to again incur the costs of the truck roll and the new platform.

The service provider would be happy to get rid of the hardware-related costs if it was possible to deliver the same service and retain the same degree of control provided by a separate physical platform. Meanwhile, PCs in the home are very powerful and could possibly be used to run the set-top box software. This situation is analogous to underutilization in the data center: multiple underutilized hardware platforms that are candidates for consolidation. Virtualization is the missing ingredient. As in the data center, virtualization can allow the set-top box to be consolidated with the PC while still providing the same level of service.

In the future, virtualization technology may be available in computers for the home. In particular, PCs designed to look like consumer electronic equipment and placed the entertainment center may eventually be capable of running many virtual machines, each with potentially different operating systems, including embedded operating systems typically used in set-top boxes. At that point, it should be possible to replace a physical set-top box by dedicating some of the entertainment PC's resources to becoming a *virtual set-top box* for a service provider.

In this scenario, the customer allows the service provider to have complete control over a virtual machine on entertainment PC. The customer first creates a virtual machine that meets the service provider's requirements for the service to be delivered. The customer creates the virtual machine to the exact specifications required by the service provider. Then, the customer delegates control of the new partition to the service provider. The provider installs the set-top box software directly into this partition, either over the network, or by delivering an installation DVD for the customer to install. The software is a standard set-top box virtual machine image from the service provider: a *set-top box software appliance*. Once installed, the service provider manages the partition-upgrading software, monitoring operation, and so on.

With the isolation between virtual machines provided by virtualization and the right access controls in place, the service provider retains the exclusive access and control over the (virtual) set-top box that it requires. The user still owns the physical machine, but the service provider "owns" and controls the set-top box partition. The service provider no longer has to deploy physical hardware to the user, saving on both the hardware itself and the associated deployment costs. Both the customer and the service provider benefit. Figure 12.2 shows the simpler scenario when a set-top box is implemented using virtualization.

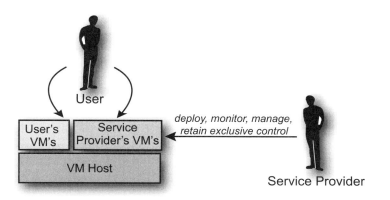

Figure 12.2   Implementing a Set-top Box Using Virtualization

Real-Time Performance Workstations

Windows-based computers are ubiquitous and have many well-established uses in the home including Web browsing, e-mail, chat, home finances, and digital photography. In addition to the more traditional uses of a home computer, people have hobbies that can require specialized and high performance hardware. For example, when playing video games, gamers want the highest performance from their PC, graphics card, and gaming peripherals. Also, when recording at home on a computer-based home recording studio, musicians must have smooth glitch-free audio for recording and playback. Some users are able to customize their own computers to eke out the required performance. Others buy from vendors that create specially tailored computers for these specific market segments. In either case, the challenge is the same: to create the highest performance system possible for the specific task.

To achieve higher performance for a given hardware platform, the most common approach is for users and manufacturers of specialized systems to attempt to "slim down" PCs to remove unnecessary software. They don't want various processes running on the host computer that aren't needed, consuming processor cycles and interfering with the primary usage. So, they remove any unnecessary applications and device drivers, attempting to make the machine as streamlined as possible. While this approach is effective to a point, it has a number of drawbacks.

- The underlying operating system is intended to be a general purpose operating system and does not provide enough end-user control to effectively strip out all unnecessary components.

- General purpose operating systems such as Windows provide no real-time performance guarantees, a feature that might be useful to many specialized embedded applications. The operating system attempts to fairly distribute access to platform resources among the active processes.

- Users would like to avoid buying new hardware. This limits their operating system choice; even though other operating systems might be more appropriate their current operating system is readily available and provides the path of least resistance. Users could configure a new operating system with a dual-boot option, but this is inconvenient and allows them to access only one operating system at a time.

- Finally, they can acquire a separate machine that is specifically built, from the ground up, for this target application, but this is most expensive option.

In the future we will be able to avoid these shortcomings by using virtualization.

First, because virtualization allows the user to run multiple operating systems simultaneously, the user has the option to select the best operating system for each application. The user (or vendor) can start with an open source operating systems and tailor it for a particular application by stripping it of all unnecessary functionality. The user has complete control over the entire stack, from operating system and device drivers to applications, and can include only the infrastructure required by the application. The user could even share the result with others in the form of a software appliance, such as an audio processing workstation.

Next, to get real-time performance guarantees, the user has the option of using an embedded operating system in any of the partitions (see the section "Utilizing Dual-core Processors for Embedded Applications" in Chapter 11), such as embedded version of the Linux, Windows CE, or another x86-based embedded operating system.

Finally, users can create performance-oriented, real-time virtual machines on the same hardware platform they use to run their general-purpose desktop operating system; no new hardware is required. In the case of a dual-core system, one core can be dedicated to running the general purpose OS VM and the other dedicated to running the real-time VM. The real-time VM, such as the audio processing workstation, is unaffected by the home user's other performance sapping programs.

Home Entertainment Center Device Consolidation

While server consolidation is the canonical example of virtualization, the principle of increasing utilization through consolidation has many applications in the home as well. The *Service Provider Partition* usage, for example, consolidates hardware from a service provider and the home user. *Real-Time Performance Workstations* consolidates the user's home computer with a specialized task-specific computer. Another potential opportunity for consolidation in the home is in the home entertainment center.

The typical home entertainment has many fixed function devices such as a CD or DVD player, tuner, amplifier, and a set-top box. The new entertainment PC, designed as consumer electronics device, is also part of this environment. As the computer industry keeps pace with Moore's Law, the processing power available continues to increase at an exponential rate and the entertainment PC will be increasingly capable of taking on more and more functionality of the other devices in the entertainment center. Many entertainment center devices will eventually be subsumed into the entertainment PC. This is starting to happen already: today's entertainment PCs can play and record CDs and DVDs, play audio received from integrated radio tuner, and can have a cable or satellite TV interface to record and playback television programs. Eventually the PC will replace the set-top box entirely. Other functions, such as the amplifier, are candidates for replacement as well. This consolidation of entertainment center device into the entertainment PC will eventually result in the PC hosting all of the functionality of the entertainment center—a more efficient use of hardware resources, with a correspondingly lower overall hardware cost.

Virtualization accelerates this trend by allowing many entertainment center components, such as the set-top box, to run as *virtual devices* in separate virtual machines on the entertainment PC. Virtual entertainment center devices provide the following benefits:

- The entertainment PC can start virtual device partitions on demand, as their services are needed.

- Because virtual machines can run embedded operating systems, if an existing physical entertainment center device is running an embedded OS, it may be relatively easy to port the device software stack to the virtual machine environment.

■ Because the virtual devices are software, they can be easily upgraded. Manufacturers can upgrade a virtual device by releasing a new virtual machine image.

■ The PC is a general purpose open system with a familiar programming environment.

Hosting Home Automation and Control

A modern home can have a surprising number of systems that can be automatically controlled, such as whole-house audio and video, home theater, lighting, heating and cooling, security, intercom, irrigation, communications, voice mail, and many more. Home automation systems allow residents to specify actions to be carried out at specific times and to define commands that control a number of devices. For example, using a home automation system, a home user could set up scenarios like the following:

■ *Watch a movie*—turn on the television, cable TV tuner, and amplifier; set the tuner to the correct channel, connect the cable TV tuner output to the TV input, dim the lights, adjust the volume, and so on. The system conveniently carries out a number of actions in response to a single command.

■ *Enable security monitoring when leaving the house*—enable various door, window, and motion sensors, as well as smoke and heat detectors. Turn off all the lights and appliances in the house and lower the temperature on the thermostat to save energy while the house is unoccupied.

Advanced scenarios like these are possible with technology on the market today, but this level of control is typically found only in more expensive high-end systems. Although many of these systems allow for PC-based control, the PC isn't yet an integral part of the overall system. In the future however, some PCs may be designed to be always on, highly reliable parts of the home infrastructure that bridge the various networks in the home—power line, telephone, home entertainment, and so on—to provide a single unified home networking platform. This kind of PC would have a high bandwidth connection to the Internet and plenty of processing power to run various monitoring, security, and control functions.

Virtualization will bring further benefits to PC-based home automation. First, isolation provided by virtual machines can make for a robust, highly available system that is worthy of hosting tasks such as home automation and home security. Next, with virtualization, a new distributed architecture is possible where virtual devices run on the home automation PC and various control points throughout the house provide the user interface that allows residents to remotely control the PC-based software. Finally, hosting the virtual devices on the PC gives the applications access to greater processing power and connectivity than running them directly on a lower-powered control panel. More sophisticated algorithms and more advanced scenarios will be possible that utilize the PC's processing power, storage capabilities, and connectivity. In addition, future home automation PCs will enable some advanced capabilities that aren't available today, like face recognition and voice response.

The Internet-connected home automation PC will enable *software-as-a-service* scenarios. Like the previous set-top box scenario discussed in this chapter, the user will be able to delegate control of a *Service Provider Partition* to an external company to allow them to install a virtual device on this partition and then monitor and control its function remotely. For example, a home security service provider could install and manage home security software into a partition on the home automation PC. The security company implements the security service using the PC-hosted virtual device and various sensors and cameras in and around the home. If the security monitoring software detects the patterns of a break-in at the residence, the company could automatically notify the police and the homeowner.

Home Health Care

Due to the rising cost of health care, there will be a continued emphasis on utilizing technology to gain efficiencies in the delivery of health-care services; not just in hospitals, but in homes as well. Home health-care scenarios will demand a computing environment with a high degree of security, reliability, and robustness.

Health Monitoring Devices

The same model used for other kinds of external service providers can be used for health care: the home user grants the health care provider access and control to a virtual machine. The provider configures and manages the new virtual machine. The partition is isolated from other virtual machines and isn't disturbed by activities in other partitions on the PC. This secure, dedicated partition can be running continuously, or on demand, as appropriate.

For example, a blood pressure monitor virtual device created and installed by the user's health care provider can run in an isolated partition on the user's PC. The virtual device interfaces to the required hardware connected to the PC to take measurements from the user. The virtual device can analyze the data locally and periodically send the data over a secure Internet link to the user's doctor. In general, using virtualization this way splits a previously monolithic device in two, moving the main application logic to a partition on the PC and leaving just the hardware required to interface to the user, as shown in Figure 12.3.

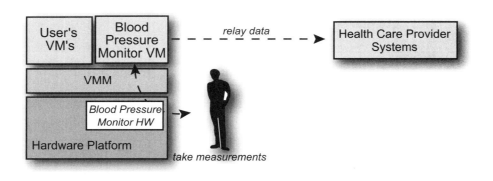

Figure 12.3   Home Health Care Virtual Machine

Products like VMware ACE allow administrators to secure the virtual machines that are running on otherwise insecure PCs. Administrators can lock down the VMs and protect the data they contain. VMware ACE also offers complete control of the virtual hardware configuration and networking capabilities of the VM. Using ACE in a health-care scenario would allow the health-care provider to create a secure virtual monitoring device partition that could run on any PC that is capable of hosting VMs.

Future Virtualization Trends

While we could continue to speculate about future usage models for virtualization, this section instead describes a few trends that seem to be emerging as a result of virtualization. In particular, continued hardware support for virtualization will eventually result in the virtualization of all platform resources, the ability to run multiple operating systems simultaneously on a single desktop, and the resulting de-emphasis of the operating system from the user's point of view. Another trend will be the ability of a PC to host multiple background virtual machines enabling networked applications that separate user input/output on various networked I/O devices from the main application logic hosted on the PC. This section suggests how these trends might unfold in the years to come.

Dynamic Allocation of Hardware Resources

VMM software will gain increasing hardware support, shrinking the performance penalty exacted to run virtual machines. In addition, other technologies, such as multi-core processors, will contribute even more processing power and enable more virtual machines to run on a single platform. Being able to freely create many low-overhead virtual machines will result in a greater emphasis on specialized virtual machines and will make them more attractive as a deployment vehicle. Whether they are called "software appliances," "virtual devices," or "dedicated partitions," the idea is the same: a developer can control the entire software stack from top to bottom—applications to operating system—which then runs in a virtual machine safely isolated from other virtual machines on the platform. The virtual device "owns" the hardware resources of the (virtual) platform and does not have to share it with other applications. This is in contrast to the traditional general purpose operating system model where the OS runs all processes on the platform and is responsible to provide fair access to platform resources. Delivering virtual devices will be appropriate for a number of applications that provide high security, reliability, and so on.

The PC will have a dynamically changing set of virtual devices running at any particular time. To facilitate dynamic loading of VMs, the VMM may require each virtual device to specify its exact hardware requirements, so that the VM gets the level of hardware support that it needs. The VMM manages the fully virtualized physical resources of the platform and allocates them to virtual machines dynamically. Virtual machine-based applications will be delivered along with their corresponding hardware requirements. The VMM will dynamically create a VM to satisfy the hardware needs of the application at load-time. Applications running in the VMs will then be able to achieve a configurable, guaranteed level of performance.

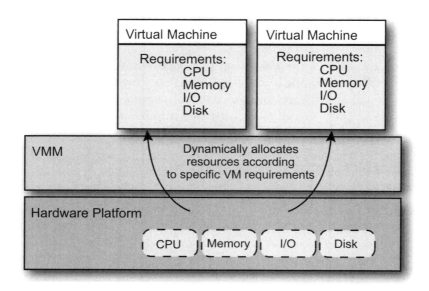

Figure 12.4 Dynamically Allocating Resources to VMs

The Fading of the Operating System

Because VMMs allow many operating systems to run simultaneously, the strong association between applications and the operating systems they require may fade for the user over time. Today, the user must make a choice about which operating system to install on a PC. In the future, many operating systems will be running simultaneously to support various applications. Applications will be bundled together with an OS as a software appliance and run automatically when the operating system is booted. When using the application, the user wouldn't really know or care about which operating system the application is using. As a result, the operating system could become more like middleware and simply provide a convenient programming environment to applications.

However, it is not clear how user interfaces will change in response to this trend. Users may not find it acceptable to be presented with many different user interface styles when running applications on various operating systems. Users' familiarity with operating system conventions and their preference for one UI style over another may keep them using a single operating system for interactive applications, using another operating system only when an application isn't available natively.

Separation of User I/O from Back-End Hardware Resources

Technologies are under development today, such as the UPnP Forum's Remote User Interface (RUI), that allow splitting an application into two parts: the user interaction front-end and the application logic back-end. A remote UI device supplies input and output services such as mouse, keyboard, and display that together comprise the user interface to an application running on a host elsewhere on the home network. Applications are matched with compatible I/O devices, and may assume different UI characteristics depending on the I/O devices used. For example, a large screen display and remote control in the family room can drive an application actually running on the PC in the den. Furthermore, the application user interface can migrate across I/O devices as the user moves about the home.

Remote UI and virtual machine technology can be combined to create easily deployed back-end applications that run on a virtual machine host. A PC can host many virtual devices simultaneously and virtual devices that are Remote UI applications will be able to provide services to user I/O devices elsewhere on the network. The virtual devices are each in separate partitions on the PC and can use the operating system that is most convenient for their implementation.

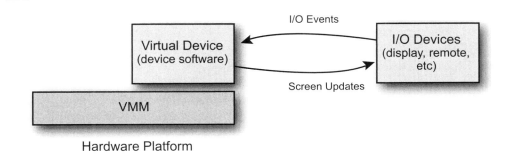

Figure 12.5   Remote I/O and Virtualization

This trend of separating user I/O and back-end application logic suggests that, eventually, a central server model could prevail in the home, where the PC takes on the role of hosting all of the application logic while the devices are reduced to reusable user interface elements. There will be many kinds of I/O devices throughout the home that could be user interface building blocks available to be driven by applications, or virtual devices, running on the PC. This will result in a greater emphasis on tailoring I/O devices for specific user experiences in the home and a greater emphasis on usability and human factors in the design of reusable I/O devices.

Conclusion

While it is fun to speculate about the future, one thing is clear: virtualization will change the status quo in computing. In this book we have attempted to present many usage models for virtualization: from known uses that companies are already taking advantage of today to reduce hardware costs, to usages that are still under development in areas such as the digital home and digital health care. Hopefully, this book has helped you to invent your own new uses for virtualization and that you are as excited about the possibilities as we are.

References

This section includes some of the various resources we drew upon to write this book, including vendor Web sites, online magazines, blogs, specifications, white papers, and books.

Technology Providers

Site	URL
Intel Virtualization Technology	www.intel.com/technology/computing/vptech/
Enterprise Virtualization and Consolidation	www.intel.com/business/bss/products/server/virtualization.htm
VMWare Home Page	www.vmware.com
XenSource Home Page	www.xensource.com/
Microsoft Virtual Server Home Page	www.microsoft.com/windowsserversystem/virtualserver/default.mspx
VMWare's Open Interfaces and Formats	www.vmware.com/interfaces/
VMWare's Community Built Virtual Appliances	www.vmware.com/vmtn/appliances/community.html

News and Information

Site	URL
Wikipedia	en.wikipedia.org/wiki/Virtualization
An Introduction to Virtualization	www.kernelthread.com/publications/virtualization/
Virtual Strategy Magazine	www.virtual-strategy.com/
Virtualization.com News Portal	www.virtualization.com/
About x86 Virtualization	about-virtualization.com/mambo/

Specifications

Site	URL
Intel® Virtualization Technology Specification for the IA-32 Intel® Architecture	ftp://download.intel.com/technology/computing/vptech/C97063-002.pdf
Intel® Virtualization Technology Specification for the Intel® Itanium® Architecture	ftp://download.intel.com/technology/computing/vptech/30594202.pdf
Intel® Virtualization Technology for Directed I/O Architecture Specification	ftp://download.intel.com/technology/computing/vptech/Intel(r)_VT_for_Direct_IO.pdf

White Papers and Articles

Site	URL
IEEE Article: Intel Virtualization Technology	ftp://download.intel.com/technology/computing/vptech/vt-ieee-computer-final.pdf
Enhanced Virtualization on Intel® Architecture-based Servers	www.intel.com/business/bss/products/server/virtualization_wp.pdf
Consolidation Strategies for Intel® Processor-based Servers	ftp://download.intel.com/business/bss/products/server/server_consolidation.pdf
Intel® Software Insight: Virtualization and Manageability	cache-www.intel.com/cd/00/00/24/28/242886_242886.pdf

Books

Muller, Al, Seburn Wilson, Don Happe, and Gary J. Humphrey, *Virtualization with VMware ESX Server,* Syngress, 2005.

Smith, James E. and Ravi Nair, *Virtual Machines: Versatile Platforms for Systems and Processes,* San Francisco, CA: Morgan Kaufmann, 2005.

Wolf, Chris and Erick M. Halter, *Virtualization: From the Desktop to the Enterprise,* Berkeley, CA: APress, 2005.

Index

66 *As the pace of technology introduction increases, it's difficult to keep up. Intel Press has established an impressive portfolio. The breadth of topics is a reflection of both Intel's diversity as well as our commitment to serve a broad technical community.*

I hope you will take advantage of these products to further your technical education. 99

Patrick Gelsinger
Senior Vice President
Intel Corporation

**Turn the page to learn about titles
from Intel Press for system developers**

Enhance security and protection against software-based attacks

The Intel Safer Computing Initiative

Building Blocks for Trusted Computing

By David Grawrock

ISBN 0-9764832-6-2

With the ever-increasing connectivity of home and business computers, it is essential that developers understand how the Intel Safer Computing Initiative can provide critical security building blocks to better protect the PC computing environment. Security capabilities need to be carefully evaluated before delivery into the marketplace. Intel is committed to delivering security capabilities in a responsible manner for end users and the ecosystem.

A highly versatile set of hardware-based security enhancements, code-named LaGrande Technology (LT), will be supported on Intel processors and chipsets to help enhance PC platforms. This book covers the fundamentals of LT and key Trusted Computing concepts such as security architecture, cryptography, trusted computer base, and trusted channels.

Highlights include:

- History of trusted computing and definitions of key concepts
- Comprehensive overview of protections that are provided by LaGrande Technology
- Case study showing how access to memory is the focal point of an attack
- Protection methods for execution, memory, storage, input, and graphics
- How the Trusted Platform Module (TPM) supports attestation

In this concise book, the lead security architect for Intel's next-generation security initiative provides critical information you need to evaluate Trusted Computing for use on today's PC systems and to prepare your designs to respond to future threats.

Managing Information Technology for Business Value

Practical Strategies for IT and Business Managers

By Martin Curley

ISBN 0-9717861-7-8

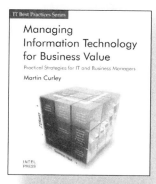

Managing Information Technology for Business Value is Martin Curley's call for IT and business managers to reformulate the way they manage IT. Curley's argument is based on evidence, from his work at Intel and with other leading enterprises, that IT investments can and should be linked directly to enterprise business indicators.

> **❝** *Curley offers practical advice and insights ... required reading for all IT executives.* **❞**
>
> *Prof. Paul Tallon,*
> *Carroll School of Management,*
> *Boston College*

Measuring the Business Value of Information Technology

Practical Strategies for IT and Business Managers

By David Sward

ISBN 0-9764832-7-0

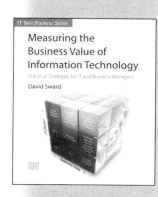

In today's fast moving competitive business environment, companies increasingly demand that IT investments demonstrate business value through measurable results. Expanding on concepts offered in Martin Curley's *Managing IT for Business Value*, David Sward explains how business value programs are established, measured, maintained, and governed, providing a blueprint for evaluating IT investments and equipping the reader with the tools required for success.

A customer-focused approach to determine the business value for any IT investment

● **Multi-Core Programming**
Increasing Performance through Software Multi-threading
By Shameem Akhter and Jason Roberts
ISBN 0-9764832-4-6

Developers can no longer rely on increasing clock speeds alone to speed up single-threaded applications; instead, to gain a competitive advantage, developers must learn how to properly design their applications to run in a threaded environment. This book helps software developers write high-performance multi-threaded code for Intel's multi-core architecture while avoiding the common parallel programming issues associated with multi-threaded programs. This book is a practical, hands-on volume with immediately usable code examples that enable readers to quickly master the necessary programming techniques.

Discover programming techniques for Intel multi-core architecture and Hyper-Threading Technology

● **The Software Optimization Cookbook, Second Edition**
High-Performance Recipes for IA-32 Platforms
By Richard Gerber, Aart J.C. Bik, Kevin B. Smith, and Xinmin Tian
ISBN 0-9764832-1-1

Four Intel experts explain the techniques and tools that you can use to improve the performance of applications for IA-32 processors. Simple explanations and code examples help you to develop software that benefits from Intel® Extended Memory 64 Technology (Intel® EM64T), multi-core processing, Hyper-Threading Technology, OpenMP†, and multimedia extensions. This book guides you through the growing collection of software tools, compiler switches, and coding optimizations, showing you efficient ways to get the best performance from software applications.

❝A must-read text for anyone who intends to write performance-critical applications for the Intel processor family.❞

Robert van Engelen,
Professor,
Florida State University

Special Deals, Special Prices!

To ensure you have all the latest books
and enjoy aggressively priced discounts,
please go to this Web site:

www.intel.com/intelpress/bookbundles.htm

Bundles of our books are available,
selected especially to address the needs
of the developer. The bundles place
important complementary topics at
your fingertips, and the price for a
bundle is substantially less than
buying all the books individually.

About Intel Press

Intel Press is the authoritative source of timely, technical books to help software and hardware developers speed up their development process. We collaborate only with leading industry experts to deliver reliable, first-to-market information about the latest technologies, processes, and strategies.

Our products are planned with the help of many people in the developer community and we encourage you to consider becoming a customer advisor. If you would like to help us and gain additional advance insight to the latest technologies, we encourage you to consider the Intel Press Customer Advisor Program. You can register here:

www.intel.com/intelpress/register.htm

For information about bulk orders or corporate sales, please send e-mail to
bulkbooksales@intel.com

Other Developer Resources from Intel

At these Web sites you can also find valuable technical information and resources for developers:

developer.intel.com	general information for developers
www.intel.com/software	content, tools, training, and the Intel® Early Access Program for software developers
www.intel.com/software/products	programming tools to help you develop high-performance applications
www.intel.com/netcomms	solutions and resources for networking and communications
www.intel.com/technology/itj	Intel Technology Journal
www.intel.com/idf	worldwide technical conference, the Intel Developer Forum

Intel
PRESS